The handbook of autism

Autism is a variable and complex developmental disorder which is frequently not recognised or else is misunderstood by both parents and professionals. *The Handbook of Autism* dispels many of the myths associated with this puzzling condition and provides readers with practical, up-to-date information.

Maureen Aarons and Tessa Gittens have worked with autistic children for over twenty years, and are convinced that parents have a right to know as much as possible about autism. By clarifying the essential issues concerning the recognition of autism, their book permits parents and professionals to reach a better mutual understanding. It enables readers to understand autism in a wider perspective, both its history and current research into possible causes; it also looks at the latest thinking on diagnosis, management and education, and on medical aspects. The authors describe their developmental approach to the assessment of autism in individual children and explore areas of special difficulty such as social understanding and communication. Case studies are used to illustrate the variability of autism, and an appendix of useful addresses is included.

Essential reading for parents of autistic children, *The Handbook of Autism* will also be immensely helpful to all professionals, in training and in practice, involved in their education and welfare.

Maureen Aarons and **Tessa Gittens** are specialist speech and language therapists working with district health authorities in the London area. Their previous book, *Is This Autism?*, was published in 1987.

The handbook of autism

A guide for parents and professionals

Maureen Aarons and Tessa Gittens

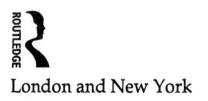

London and New York

First published 1992
by Routledge
11 New Fetter Lane, London EC4P 4EE

Simultaneously published in the USA and Canada
by Routledge
29 West 35th Street, New York, NY 10001

Reprinted 1994

A Tavistock/Routledge publication

Typeset in Times by Michael Mepham, Frome, Somerset
Printed and bound in Great Britain by
Biddles Ltd, Guildford and King's Lynn

British Library Cataloguing in Publication Data
A catalogue record for this book is available from the British Library

Library of Congress Cataloging in Publication Data
A catalog record for this book is available from the Library of Congress

ISBN 0-415-05565-2 (hbk)
ISBN 0-415-05566-0 (pbk)

To the parents who read *Is This Autism?* and offered helpful suggestions which were the basis for this book

Contents

Authors' note

Please note that, for consistency of style, the pronoun 'he' is used throughout the book. The authors do not want to be considered sexist in their choice of the masculine pronoun, which was chosen because there is a marked predominance of male autistic children.

Foreword

Maureen Aarons and Tessa Gittens have long experience of working with children with disorders in the autistic continuum and
their families. They understand the nature of autism and the distress caused to the parents by their children's developmental
delays and strange behaviour. They recognise and empathise with
the uncertainty and worry felt by parents before they know the
reasons for their child's problems, and the shock and misery when
they are told the diagnosis. They spell out clearly the long-term
nature of the disabilities but they are equally clear that a great deal
can be done by parents and professionals to help the children cope
better with a world which they find so puzzling.

The authors give special attention to the problems of definition
of autistic disorders and the need to recognise the underlying
impairments in all the different ways whereby they can be manifested in overt behaviour. They also discuss the reluctance of some
professional workers to use the word autism. Naming somehow
gives substance and reality to previously vague fears. There is an
episode in *Alice Through the Looking Glass* in which Alice enters the
wood where things have no names. She meets a fawn and they
walk through the wood side by side because neither knows who
or what the other is. As they leave the wood, the fawn realises that
it *is* a fawn and that Alice is a human being, so it darts away in
alarm. When I was a child, I loved the drawing of Alice with her
arm round the neck of the baby deer and felt very sad when reality
spoilt the picture. As an adult and a parent, I experienced the same
sad transition from ignorance to painful knowledge when our
daughter's difficulties were identified and named as autism. For a
time it seemed that the whole world had become grey and empty

but we slowly picked up the pieces and sought for constructive ways to help our child and, in doing so, also helped ourselves.

In those days – the late 1950s – little was known about autism. In 1962 we joined with a small group of parents to become the founder members of the Society for Autistic Children, now called the National Autistic Society. We were full of determination and firmly believed that autistic children were not mentally retarded, and that their isolated, idiosyncratic abilities were the true indicators of their future potential. We did not believe the more guarded predictions of the few professionals who had had long experience in the field. We saw what some gifted teachers could achieve with some children. We did not recognise the difference between rote learning and true understanding, so we thought that appropriate education would cure all the problems and not just help to diminish them, as we know now. Because the concept of autism had been formulated only 20 years earlier, we did not know any parents of adults diagnosed as autistic who could tell us what the future might hold.

Now, as the authors describe, the situation is quite different. The National and Local Autistic Societies have many members with grown up sons and daughters. The parents of young children with autism have access to knowledge about the probable future that was denied to us founder members. It is clear that typical autism is just one sub-group in a continuum of disorders involving social and communication impairments that are lifelong in their effects, although they vary in their severity from profound to minimal and subtle but still detectable. Eventual outcome is determined more by the overall level of ability of the child than by any method of treatment. However, it is equally clear that, however severe the disabilities, a great deal can be done by parents and professional workers in collaboration to help make life more satisfying and pleasant for those affected. Furthermore, most families find that there are many compensations in the long run despite all the difficulties, not least a more realistic appreciation of what is important in life and what is trivial. Parents of all children enjoy seeing their child progress, but for parents of autistic children each small step in development brings a special pleasure.

However, as the authors warn, it takes time for the pain brought by knowledge to fade into a quiet sadness in the background and the development of an accepting but positive attitude. During this time, parents are vulnerable to all kinds of pressures, including promises of cures or, at the very least, major changes for the better, from those with a variety of different theories. For the founder members, very little was on offer; now there is a plethora of promises. There is also, of course, the desire to deny the diagnosis and to seek other explanations of the impairments of social interaction, communication and imagination with which professional workers sometimes collude. As I am a professional in the field as well as a parent, I know at first hand the emotional stress experienced by anyone who has to tell parents that their child is autistic. However many times you have had to do this, it becomes no easier. It is made even harder by the natural human tendency to blame the messenger for the message.

The vivid accounts of individual children in this book illustrate that all people with autistic disorders share the same underlying impairments, but that each child and his or her family is different. A professional worker, faced with breaking the news, must assess how much the parents know or suspect already and how much of the truth they can bear at any one time – no easy task. Diagnosis must include a detailed assessment of each child's pattern of skills and disabilities and the information explained to the parents in a way that is acceptable to them. It is absolutely necessary to be honest about the limitations of knowledge, to explain the pitfalls of diagnosis and assessment, and to allow for the possibility of a change of opinion as events unfold over the years. Ideally, there should be ample opportunity for return visits to discuss the diagnosis and its implications for the child concerned, and local support for the family should be arranged. In practice, there are constraints on the resources available. Nevertheless, I know from long experience that it is only when the truth is faced that healing of the emotional wounds can begin and constructive action planned and undertaken. Parents of older children and adults always say that, looking back, they would have wanted to be told the truth about their children as early as possible, however much this would have distressed them at the time. Of course, events always appear in a different light when viewed in retrospect.

The authors are clear-sighted, honest and positive in their approach. Their book is for parents, the great majority, who have the courage to emerge from the spurious comfort of the wood where things have no names and begin to take up the challenge. Their life will be different from how they had planned it but can be full of the satisfaction of difficulties overcome and the friendship, wherever they go in the world, of those who have lived through the same experience.

Lorna Wing

Introduction

The writing of this book was the outcome of not only twenty years experience as speech and language therapists working with autistic children and their families, but also, more specifically, because of a surge in the number of referrals in the districts in which we were working. These were very young children and our many encounters with their parents had the effect of sharpening our understanding of what they were going through and awareness of their needs.

There is a particular poignancy about the diagnosis of autism. Typically, these children look so attractive and normal that it is all too easy to ignore or dismiss the signs and symptoms and concentrate instead on the singular, often curious skills or islets of ability which the children frequently display. There was a remarkable consistency in the sort of questions that the parents asked, and the sort of information that they required as they attempted to come to terms with the complexities of the diagnosis. The realisation that the nature of their child's handicap was more serious than they may have anticipated was the first reality to be faced. This dilemma was often exacerbated by the fact that other professionals might have offered different explanations for the problems the child presented.

Some individual parents expressed the difficulties caused by well-intentioned relatives, including grandparents, who denied the existence of any real problems with assurances that the child would 'grow out of it'. Others, less kindly, blamed the parents by seeing the child's problems in terms of neglect or mismanagement. The most difficult situations existed where the parents of the child took opposing views.

Until quite recently, our response to parents' questioning had been positive encouragement to contact the National Autistic Society for information and support, and generally this continues to be our practice. However, we were made very aware that, for many parents, even telephoning the Society, never mind joining, implied an acceptance of the diagnosis or label of autism which they were not ready to make.

Apart from the excellent information provided by the Society, there are very few books on autism available in shops and libraries for the 'lay' reader. Newspaper reports and television features appear from time to time, but tend to promote miracle cures which are good for media purposes but are unsubstantiated and misleading. We hope this book will fill the gap between the miracle cures and the more 'academic' publications.

Our aim is to provide non-specialist readers, be they parents, nursery nurses, playgroup leaders, psychologists, teachers, speech and language therapists and others, with up-to-date information which covers such matters as diagnosis, research, management and education, as well as medical considerations in relation to autism. Whereas, in the past, autism was presented as a discrete condition – something enclosed in a circle with precise boundaries – we now see it on a continuum – a line stretching from severely affected individuals to those whose abnormalities are very mild and indeed fade into eccentric normality. For this reason, a diagnosis of autism need not inevitably imply doom and gloom. Some children, albeit a small number, make very good progress and may even cope with mainstream education. In this book we will generally refer to more severely affected children, as their problems are more wide-ranging. Parents of children at the upper end of the continuum, while recognising some aspects of the more overtly autistic, may experience very few, if any, of their management problems and yet be puzzled by their child's development and behavioural oddities. We are aware of this, yet believe that this book will be of equal use to them.

Most parents, when they learn that their child is autistic, are anxious to help in a practical way. They abhor the feeling of helplessness when nothing seems to be happening and no specialised help and support is available. In Chapter 6 we have included some practical suggestions and advice, which we hope will go some way towards alleviating these feelings of frustration. In addition we have included two appendices. The first consists of case histories, because we often find that parents better understand their child's difficulties if they see them mirrored in accounts of other children. The second aims to provide parents with general information and advice, as well as some useful addresses. At the end of the book there is a list of references and further reading.

As speech and language therapists, we are aware that it is the lack of development of language in children, later diagnosed as autistic, which causes most concern to parents. For this reason we are often the first professionals to see young autistic children. The expectation is that, by some means, we will provide them with meaningful speech and all will be well. It is a heavy responsibility for the speech and language therapist to disappoint parents by demonstrating that the child's problems are wider ranging, and not confined to speech and language alone.

Our experience centres around young autistic children. Although we include a chapter on autism in adolescence and adulthood (Chapter 9, Growing up – what lies beyond?), in general their problems and needs are beyond the scope of this book.

We must not end this Introduction without attempting to reach those parents who have been told that their child is autistic, yet cannot accept that it is an appropriate or justified diagnosis. They may feel that the very word has extreme associations and is a 'label' which can only have a negative effect on their child's future. It may be that this book has been picked up in the hope that autism can once and for all be excluded. Perhaps considerable anger is felt towards the professional who suggested the diagnosis. How was it possible to reach such a conclusion in what may have seemed such a very short time? Some parents feel that the diagnosis was presented in the wrong way, or that perversely, the professional's great knowledge of the condition predisposed their thinking. Others may feel that they inadvertently let their child down by disclosing developmental details which precipitated the diagnosis. It is not unusual for parents themselves to suggest a diagnosis of autism, yet when the professional confirms this, believing perhaps that the parents have come to terms with the notion, there may be unexpected repercussions. Confirmation of their own worst fears is the last thing they want to hear and their subsequent reactions are no different from those of parents who are unaware of the nature of their child's difficulties.

The autistic specialist is in a catch-22 situation, and it is almost impossible to do the right thing. If too little is said, the professional is likely to be found wanting for a number of reasons. Parents may feel that valuable time has been wasted when they could have obtained appropriate help and support. Suitable schools could have been investigated and their child's name put on waiting lists when necessary. More importantly perhaps, parents wanting the best for their child are likely to go on seeking a diagnosis and while doing so, possibly feel guilty and confused. Much time and money may be expended as the quest continues.

It is important for parents not to feel that the person offering the diagnosis is somehow 'the opposition', to be fought against and argued with. Of course we do not live in a perfect world, but there should be a feeling of partnership and shared objectives, as issues are explored and appropriate and acceptable actions are taken.

We hope that this book will help to clarify the essential issues in relation to the recognition of autism and thereby permit better understanding between parents and professionals.

Chapter 1

The variable picture of autism

Autism, with its paradoxical signs and symptoms, is a comparatively rare condition which fascinates to such an extent that the majority of the population have an idea of what it is without having had any direct contact with an autistic individual. The success of the film *Rainman* with Dustin Hoffman, added to the public's awareness of autism, yet it portrayed only one particular manifestation of the condition.

Most people if asked 'what is autism?' are able to give an opinion covering a wide range of ideas:

They're withdrawn . . . they can't communicate . . . they're very musical . . . they're very good at maths . . . they're very clever . . . they're all mentally handicapped.

These simplistic and disparate views reflect some of the extensive variations which exist in the condition. In order to illustrate the variability of autism, we shall describe two individual children. Both are very different from each other, yet both are autistic. The common thread that links them will be explained in the next chapter, when the causes of the condition of autism will be discussed.

Lucy is an alert and very attractive 4½-year-old who looks entirely normal. She is physically well co-ordinated and dances with pleasure and grace. Occasionally she will be seen to observe objects from odd angles and to lie on the floor in order to do this. Although she does not appear to seek out physical contact and cuddles, she shows no physical avoidance. Her eye contact, which was previously poor, would not now be regarded as abnormal and there is no gaze avoidance. Lucy's play seems well developed when first observed. She enjoys water and sand, spends time in the home corner and is always busy and occupied. However, although her play appears purposeful and meaningful, it has a repetitive quality and shows no development. In addition, she does not draw other children into her activities. There is a quality of 'separateness' about her which singles her out from other children. Her attention is poor, unless it centres around her own interests. In self-care skills she is very capable and her cognitive abilities appear appropriate for her age. Evidently, Lucy has artistic abilities. Her painting is impressive, as is her modelling, but both are repetitive. She shows great reluctance to extend her repertoire or to develop these skills as her capabilities suggest. Although Lucy's hearing is completely normal, she is very likely not to respond when her name is called or when she is spoken to. It is not possible to have a conversation with her and any attempts at a two-way dialogue meet with little success. However, Lucy talks a great deal, commenting on her own activities as well as making statements which, although perfectly articulated and grammatically complex, generally show little relevance to the situation. This feature is known as delayed echolalia: when phrases and sentences are repeated some time after they have been heard. Lucy did not acquire speech and language at the normal age, and for this reason was referred to speech and language therapy for assessment, where it was considered that she had an unusual disorder of language. It was not until she was over four years old that autism was diagnosed.

The second child, David, who is now 6½ years old, is also attractive. He is a smiling and happy child with a gaze that is often unfocused. His eye contact is fleeting, unless centred on objects that are of interest to him. These objects range from television and video screens, to insignificant details of pictures in books, which he scrutinises with great pleasure. David's physical development appeared normal, although certain oddities such as tiptoe walking, were observed when he was about 3 years old. He now appears physically immature. His habit of sucking his tongue, together with hands which are constantly writhing and flapping, present a picture of oddity so that, in a group of normal children, he would stand out. In contrast to Lucy's indifference to physical contact, David seeks out cuddles from his mother and has to be dissuaded from touching and feeling any exposed female flesh, as well as from gazing with rapt attention at stockinged legs. Apart from the interests described, and some willingness to complete jigsaws, David will not engage in any meaningful activities and could best be described as a 'loller', in contrast to Lucy's constant busyness. He shows no awareness of danger and, when taken to the park, is likely to 'do a runner' unless kept on a tight rein. Other inappropriate aspects of his development are a refusal to use a toilet standing up, and to eat only a very limited selection of food. When spoken to, David may or may not respond. Generally he does not use speech, although he is capable of producing words and phrases largely in response to his own needs. He is not interested in communication, but mutters and sometimes makes 'whooping' noises for no apparent reason. Occasionally short inappropriate and meaningless phrases are uttered, for example 'go on the District Line', but these are rare and in no way compare with Lucy's expressive abilities. Coupled with this picture of deviant development and abnormal behaviour, David's learning abilities (or cognitive skills) are very limited, and indeed do not differ from any child with severe learning difficulties.

Our descriptions of the distinctive characteristics of Lucy and David illustrate the wide-ranging nature of autism. Although the diagnosis may explain the confusing pattern of developmental difficulties, every autistic child is autistic in his/her own particular way. Indeed, they are as individual as normal children. In Chapter 2 we shall discuss the concept of autism existing on a continuum of severity. The differing profiles presented by Lucy and David will then make better sense.

Chapter 2

The history of autism

In order to understand autism it is necessary to look at it historically. The condition was first described by Kanner in 1943. He listed a number of features which, in theory, would identify children with this disorder. His use of the term 'autistic' caused some confusion right from the start because it had previously been used in connection with the withdrawal into fantasy shown by schizophrenics. At that time it appeared to afflict children of well-educated parents in the upper socio-economic classes, but this is more likely to reflect referral bias than clinical fact.

It is worth listing these points, because they are still relevant and show the condition in its 'classic' form:

1 *An inability to develop relationships*
   This means that an autistic child will have difficulty interacting with people and is likely to show more interest in objects rather than other human beings.

2 *Delay in the acquisition of language*
   Although some autistic children remain mute, others do acquire language, but almost invariably it appears considerably later than in children with normal development.

3 *Non-communicative use of spoken language after it develops*
   This describes a peculiarity which is characteristic of autistic children. In spite of having adequate words at their disposal, they have difficulty in using them in meaningful conversation.

4 *Delayed echolalia*
   This is the repetition of words and phrases which is very common in autistic children.

5 *Pronominal reversal*
This means simply that the child substitutes 'you' for 'I'. For example: Parent: Do you want a biscuit? Child: You want a biscuit.

6 *Repetitive and stereotyped play*
Typically, the play of autistic children is very limited. They tend to repeat the same activity and do not develop imaginative pretend play.

7 *Maintenance of sameness*
This describes the insistence shown by many autistic children in resisting changes in their surroundings and daily lives.

8 *Good rote memory*
Many autistic children show remarkable feats of memory and rote learning.

9 *Normal physical appearance*
It was this last feature which encouraged Kanner to believe that autistic children invariably had normal intelligence, an impression that has only comparatively recently been discounted.

Kanner later reduced these points to two essential features:

1 Maintenance of sameness in children's repetitive routines.

2 Extreme aloneness, with onset within the first two years.

This reduction caused even more confusion, as many children, while clearly showing a pattern of difficulties, did not fit these criteria which picked out only cases of classic autism.

At about the same time an Austrian psychiatrist, Hans Asperger, independently recognised a pattern of abnormal behaviour in a group of adolescents, which he chose to call an autistic 'psychopathy' – that is an abnormality of personality. As Asperger wrote in German during war years, his work, with detailed clinical descriptions, is less widely known and has not been fully understood. In fact, those familiar with German have indicated that Asperger and Kanner both describe the same condition. Digby Tantam, in his National Autistic Society publication, *A Mind of One's Own*, suggests that a sub-group exists of 'autistic people who are sociable, highly clumsy, verbally skilled and with highly developed special interests'. He uses the term 'Asperger's Syndrome' to define individuals with this cluster of difficulties. In our experience, the label has come to be a useful shorthand for describing more able autistic people. However, debate continues about the existence of subtle distinctions between the two conditions. The publication of *Autism and Asperger Syndrome*, edited by Uta Frith, should clarify at least some of the issues.

Since that time, other researchers have listed their own criteria, and for a number of years it was usual to diagnose autism by counting up a requisite number of points. The weakness of such a system must be obvious. A child could have eight features out of nine, and would be declared 'not autistic'. However, in recent years, as researchers have gained a better understanding of the condition, a more common-sense approach is becoming established among clinicians.

Professor Michael Rutter, of the Institute of Psychiatry, has contributed considerably to the understanding of autism as well as language disability, and has led the way towards a more cohesive view of the condition. Although he too listed points, they were more broadly based. Rutter acknowledged variations in intelligence and suggested that IQ was as relevant to autistic as to non-autistic children. This was important because it shifted the focus away from the assumption that autistic children were invariably of normal intelligence, which Kanner had suggested.

Dr Elizabeth Newson of Nottingham University enlarged on Rutter's criteria. Whereas he referred to 'delay and deviant language development', she referred to 'impairment in all modes of communication', which included facial expression and gesture. Both Rutter and Newson reiterated Kanner's reference to 'the age of onset'. With better understanding of the nature of autism, this point now seems less significant. What they regarded as 'age of onset' may have been the age when the condition was finally recognised in the child.

This accumulation of knowledge about autism showed that it was not invariably a clear-cut disorder like measles, which you either have or have not got, but a spectrum of difficulties with certain clusters of possible symptoms.

We feel that the descriptive definition suggested by Dr Lorna Wing, formerly of the Medical Research Council Social Psychiatry Unit, makes best sense of this complex condition. She, together with a colleague, Dr Judith Gould, carried out an epidemiological study of children resident within a particular area of London in

1979. They included in the study any child with autistic features, as well as all children who were severely mentally handicapped. This study led them to suggest that the core deficit in autism is *social* in nature. This means that whereas a mentally handicapped child can be sociable, relative to his/her mental age, an autistic child, regardless of intellectual ability, will have observable social impairments. These difficulties, apparent in three different areas of functioning, were described as 'The Triad of Impairments of Social Interaction'. When describing them, Wing, in her most recent work following up the original children (now well into adolescence), underlines the idea that autism is on a continuum. This means that there is no clearly defined limit to the disorder. The continuum can include all the 'odd' and atypical children who clinicians constantly come across, who do not fall strictly into the classic picture of autism as described by Kanner. Social deficits have invariably been mentioned by other researchers. Wing and Gould's work has highlighted them as being central to the disorder.

The three aspects of the Triad are:

1   An impairment of social relationships.

2   An impairment of social communication.

3   An impairment of social understanding and imagination.

We need to look at each of these areas in more detail and, for the sake of clarity, we have listed below the points or levels on the continuum suggested by Wing. The lower numbers describe more severely handicapped children. More able autistic children may be identified by the descriptions listed under (4) in each of the areas of the Triad. However, it should be borne in mind that the levels listed are arbitrary and that, in practice, children will be found who are functioning at any point along the way.

IMPAIRMENT OF SOCIAL RELATIONSHIPS

1   Aloofness and indifference to others.

2   Accepting of social approaches by others (passive).

3   Makes social approaches to others which are one-sided, and may be to indulge strange and unusual interests, e.g. railway timetables, vacuum cleaners, lavatory disinfectants, X-ray scanners, broken park benches, etc.

4   Makes social contact, but lacks understanding of subtle rules of social behaviour.

IMPAIRMENT OF SOCIAL COMMUNICATION

1   Absence of any desire to communicate with others.

2   Communication confined to the expression of needs only.

3   Makes factual comments, not part of a social exchange, and often irrelevant to the social context.

4   Talks a great deal, but regardless of response of listeners, and does not engage in reciprocal conversation.

IMPAIRMENT OF SOCIAL UNDERSTANDING AND IMAGINATION

1   Copying and pretend play are absent.

2   May copy the actions of others, but without real understanding of their meaning and purpose (may bath doll, etc.).

3   Repetitive and stereotyped enacting of a role, but without variation or empathy, e.g. a TV character or even an object such as an aeroplane.

4   Awareness that something goes on in the minds of others, but has no strategies to discover what this may be. (Minimally impaired people appear to have ability to recognise others' feelings, but this is learnt rather than empathetic.)

Wing links the behavioural abnormalities seen in autistic children with these levels of social functioning. While lower functioning children frequently display abnormal responses to sensory stimuli, together with odd movements such as flapping, the least severely handicapped are more likely to display a special skill which is at a level beyond their chronological age.

The practicalities of how the Triad affects a child's development will, we hope, become clearer as we describe and discuss the assessment of autistic children in Chapter 5. In the natural history of the disorder, improvements and changes are likely to take place. For example, the unsociable child may become sociable in a passive way, and the passive child may become sociable but odd. It is necessary to clarify the differences between impaired and immature social development. While children with impaired social development will display some or all of the idiosyncratic patterns described, the socially immature child will display a more normal profile which will relate to their overall developmental level, rather than their chronological age.

Wing has also contributed to the debate on the existence of Asperger's Syndrome. She has described a sub-group of individuals who:

1   Make naive and inappropriate social approaches.

2   Have narrow circumscribed interests.

3   Have poor motor co-ordination.

4   Have long-winded repetitive speech.

5   Have no common sense.

There has been considerable argument about what underlies the varied picture that autism presents. Why is a child who has only a few of Kanner's features autistic? What has such a child in common with one more obviously and seriously handicapped? Is there a common thread? What is the link?

Uta Frith, a research psychologist at the Medical Research Council Cognitive Development Unit, in her recently published book entitled *Autism: Explaining the Enigma*, has made a considerable contribution to answering these questions. It is very satisfactory to be able to relate our two decades of clinical experience of observing and assessing dozens of autistic children, to the theoretical model suggested by her research. Her experimental work is based on Premack's 'Theory of Mind'. This is the ability to attribute mental states with content to others (mentalising). Frith has postulated that it is the ability to mentalise that is lacking in autistic individuals. We will be referring to this deficit in later chapters, when we look at the practical aspects of assessing autistic children. The final paragraph of her book sums up simply and coherently what parents and professionals with experience of autism will immediately recognise:

To identify the core features we had to look below the surface of the symptoms. It was then that we could see the red thread that was running through the evidence. It is the inability to draw together information so as to derive coherent and meaningful ideas. There is a fault in the predisposition of the mind to make sense of the world. Just this particular fault in the mechanics of the mind can explain the essential features of autism. If we lose sight of this fact, we lose sight of the overall pattern.

Having described the historical background to autism from 1943 to the present day, it is appropriate to touch upon the establishment of The National Autistic Society in this country. The motivation to form a Society came originally from a group of parents of autistic children. The Society celebrated its twenty-fifth anniversary in 1987. One of its original aims was to set up schools for autistic children who were, in 1962, excluded from the limited facilities provided by education and health authorities for handicapped children. It was then agreed by the Society that no autistic child should be excluded from their schools. The Society schools continue to flourish. They are located in different parts of the country, and although not identical in terms of what is offered, do provide a model of excellence, both in educational approaches and management of associated problems. Over the years, these schools have achieved much success with individual children. Their work continues, unendorsed by media attention, yet establishing standards of care which are respected internationally. The lack of post-school provision for older children and young adults is a matter of concern to the Society, and steps are being taken to remedy this situation. The role of the National Autistic Society has grown over the years but it remains a parent-oriented organisation. As a result of renewed interest in 'alternative' approaches to autism, the Society now accepts that it has a role to play in the evaluation of the claims that are made by their proponents. Their appraisals provide parents with information about any possible benefits, as well as disadvantages in terms of location, financial costs and possible effects on other siblings in the family. These different approaches will be described in some greater detail in Chapter 10, A postscript – alternative treatments and cures for autism?.

As well as encouraging the formation of locally based support groups, the Society organises conferences and study days for both parents and professionals. In addition it publishes books, pamphlets and reports, as well as a regular newsletter. It provides an information service and, more generally, promotes better awareness and understanding of autism. A recent innovation is the establishment of the Asperger's Syndrome Support Network, which focuses on the particular problems of more able autistic people. A database of publications and research information has been established by the Society at Sunderland Polytechnic. A directory is available and is primarily geared to the needs of professionals in the field of autism. It will, however, also be possible for parents to obtain this information. A very welcome extension of the Society's services, is the decision to establish a diagnostic centre which, although based in the South East, will provide a much needed focus for increasing and developing diagnostic expertise.

There have been two Government-funded research projects which have investigated aspects of provision and outcome for autistic children and young adults. The first, in 1984, considered the position of able autistic people in society. The second, which at the time of writing is on-going, has a wider brief and was established to 'describe the facilities currently available for autistic children and adults provided by the public, private and voluntary sectors in England and Wales and to study in detail some of the methods used to address the particular problems of autism'. The latter project is based at the Child Development Research Unit at the University of Nottingham. The team has already produced a paper entitled 'Autistic Children in Ordinary Mainstream Schools'. It is to be hoped this will be followed by further equally informative reports.

With the prospect of ever-increasing movement, not only between the countries of Europe but also the rest of the world, it is likely that some parents of autistic children will settle abroad. Naturally the attitudes towards diagnosis and the provision for autistic children will vary considerably from country to country. There are two standardised classification systems for psychiatric diseases and disabilities that are used internationally. Both have sections on autistic disorders. Each is updated every few years. One is produced by the American Psychiatric Association and is called the Diagnostic and Statistical Manual of Mental Disorders (DSM) and the latest version is the third revised edition (DSM-III-R). The other is produced by the World Health Organisation and is called the International Classification of Diseases (ICD). This covers physical as well as psychiatric disorders. The latest edition is the tenth (ICD-10).

The significant changes in the sections dealing with autistic disorders in succeeding editions of these classification systems, illustrate the changes in perception of the nature of autism and the continuing debate about diagnosis. The latest editions of both, recognise a range of sub-groups of autistic disorders that is wider than classic autism and which both call 'pervasive developmental disorders' (PDD). These are roughly equivalent to the continuum of disorders in which Wing's 'triad of social and communication impairments' occur. While it is of interest to researchers to investigate and carefully define sub-groups within the autistic continuum, it can lead to a proliferation of labels which is likely to confuse rather than clarify diagnosis. It is important to recognise the social and communication impairments in all developmental areas, and then to assess each child's own pattern of skills and deficits.

Clearly, it is not feasible to write a description of the state-of-the-art in each and every country. However, the National Autistic Society can provide a comprehensive list of autistic societies and contacts throughout most of the world.

Chapter 3

What causes autism?

We hope that the descriptions of the developments in the understanding of autism outlined in the previous chapter will enable readers to appreciate the variations and subtleties of the condition. We know that a medical model, that is defining autism as a disease, may not be helpful. Instead, it is more appropriate to view it in terms of a socio-educational disorder. This encourages the use of the term in a contextual sense, rather than as a rigid label. In our view it would be unhelpful to abandon the use of the term altogether, as it is an appropriate framework of reference for recognising and understanding a group of children who show unusual and contradictory patterns of development.

Since Kanner's time, many theories have been suggested to account for autism and the possible causes. Initially, it was believed that the parents were at fault, particularly the mother who was held responsible for not providing sufficient warmth and affection for her child. Commonly used phrases were 'refrigerator mother' and 'cold intellectual parents'. Fortunately, such ill-founded and critical views became discredited as clinical experience and research repudiating these theories developed. However, recently there has been a revival of a similar hypothesis, which is based on a theory propounded by Tinbergen and Tinbergen in 1972. They claimed that autism is caused by a breakdown in the bonding process between mother and child, and that this theory provides the basis for a cure. The idea was taken up with great enthusiasm by Dr Martha Welch, an American psychiatrist. She introduced what is known as 'holding therapy'. This is not, as we originally supposed, a warm and cosy cuddling dialogue, but a forced hold of the child by the mother which has to be maintained, despite resistance by the child, and involves much struggling, crying and shouting. The tenor of holding therapy sessions, which we have seen on video, appears to us to be quasi-religious, and the fervour generated caused us considerable disquiet. It is impossible to see how such 'therapy' could possibly cure (as it is claimed) a condition such as autism. The lack of evaluation and assessment by the providers of this therapy, does little to substantiate their claims, which can therefore only be considered as anecdotal. There is ample scientific evidence that during the middle years of childhood, from about six years until adolescence, many autistic children make considerable spontaneous improvement. Autistic features may diminish and progress can occur in a number of areas in relation to social development, language and educational attainments (see Appendix 2: Case studies). In the gentler and less aggressive setting of schools with expertise and understanding, autistic children will have the opportunity to develop their full potential on a realistic basis. The dramatic claims of a cure will not be made because, however much progress occurs, the underlying core deficits will remain and need to be taken into account. As we later expand on the various aspects of the autistic continuum, it should become obvious why this simplistic and unscientific remedy is ill-conceived and inappropriate. However, over the years we have met several mothers who, despite all evidence to the contrary, insist that their child's autistic condition is caused by them. Women with these feelings of intractible guilt are more likely to be drawn towards this theory, and no amount of reasoning is likely to alter their belief.

Holding therapy is just one of a number of so-called 'cures' for autism which emerge from time to time in the media. As none have been substantiated, it would seem neither useful nor appropriate for us to explore them in depth, but we will describe them briefly in the last chapter of this book. Understandably, parents will want to have their hopes raised, however tenuous the evidence, but they should be encouraged to maintain a sceptical attitude until some evaluated data provides them with realistic expectations. All the evidence now available strongly indicates that the causes of autism are biological. Contrary to Kanner's original assumption, epidemiological studies now indicate that autism affects children born into all strata of society, without regard to intellectual or socio-economic factors, or ethnic origins.

The National Autistic Society confirms that the incidence of autism is 4 or 5:10,000 for classic cases, and 17:10,000 for closely related conditions which will require similar services. These figures are higher than earlier estimations quoted in the literature. However, more recently still, researchers looking at the full spectrum of autistic disorders have suggested that the incidence may be as high as 23:10,000.

Those familiar with autism will know that there are more autistic boys than girls. Although the exact ratios vary, autistic males tend to outnumber females by 3 or 4:1. This prevalence of males over females, together with the known association of autism with severe mental retardation, provides further evidence that the causes of the condition are not psychogenic in origin.

Recent research has shown that not only do relatives of autistic people stand a slightly greater than average chance of being autistic, but that autistic people's families have an unusually high percentage of relatives with speech disorders, learning difficulties and other minor cognitive disabilities. There have been a number of studies of identical and non-identical twins where one or both are affected by autism. These have provided important information relating to genetic factors. In addition to the twin studies, researchers are also looking at autistic children who were adopted before a diagnosis of autism was made. Some of this research is on-going and it is hoped that the outcome will further clarify the aetiology of the condition.

For some time certain physical disorders have been known to be associated with autism. These include maternal rubella, infantile spasms and untreated phenylketonuria. In addition, autism is also linked to known inherited disorders such as tuberous sclerosis, neurofibromatosis and fragile X-syndrome. Rett's syndrome is another recent addition to this list. Recent research has also indicated that certain viruses, as well as rubella, may be implicated in the causation of autism. In particular, the *herpes simplex* virus as well as the *cytomegalo* virus have been mentioned in the literature. Even *candida albicans*, a common yeast-like fungus causing thrush, has been linked with autism. Interestingly, a significant number of parents have reported unexplained high temperatures or transient rashes in their autistic children. Is this perhaps evidence of yet another active virus? Recent experience leads us to believe that cases of autism are on the increase, which cannot be simply explained by increased awareness of the condition. There is an interesting theory that a virus can infect a baby *in utero*, but it will be only minimally damaged and appear normal at birth. Yet the virus may be dormant in the child and can be activated by the normal stresses of life, such as moving house, the birth of another child, etc. This theory provides a possible explanation for the many reports by parents that their previously normal child *became* autistic having had these experiences. It is not uncommon for autistic children to suffer from epilepsy, although sometimes its onset is delayed until adolescence. This association between the two conditions indicates the presence of overt organic brain dysfunction and again provides evidence of a biological basis for autism. In general, severely handicapped autistic children are more likely to suffer from epilepsy than those at the upper end of the continuum, but this is by no means universal.

About one-third of autistic children tested in various studies have raised levels of blood serotonin. However, treatment with the drug fenfluramine, aimed at reducing these levels and accordingly the autistic symptoms, has not proved to be generally effective and remains experimental. Similarly, the use of vitamin therapy as well as other pharmacological agents such as folic acid, magnesium and zinc, have not proved to be any more successful. It is to be hoped that continuing research may yield improved results in the future.

It seems very likely that brain damage or dysfunction is present in autism in all its manifestations. Obviously where there is severe social impairment, mental retardation and physical difficulties, the extent of the damage will be considerably greater than in cases where there is social impairment, but where many skill areas are intact. There has been much speculation about the parts of the brain which are affected in autism and particular areas of interest have included the right hemisphere; recent research in the United States has found abnormalities in parts of the cerebellum. However, as yet, no single area of the brain has been conclusively implicated, which could account for the wide range of presenting features, and it seems much more likely that multiple neurological deficits exist.

Dr Christopher Gillberg of the Child Neuropsychiatry Centre, Göteborg, Sweden, has written an excellent and informative paper which reviews the most interesting recent research in the field of autism. This paper is listed in *References and further reading*.

Perhaps Dr Sula Wolff of Edinburgh University makes sense of all the diverse aetiological factors by suggesting that

for autism to develop, brain damage has to occur in the setting of a genetic predisposition . . . the causation of autism which is likely to be heterogeneous, arises when a number of possibly quite common factors coincide and it is the coincidence which is rare and makes autism uncommon.

Chapter 4

Problems of diagnosis

The National Autistic Society describes autism as a mental handicap, a statement which requires clarification, because in fact a small number of autistic individuals are not intellectually impaired in the usual sense. Intelligence tests have shown that approximately 60 per cent of autistic children have IQ scores of below 50, 20 per cent between 50 and 70, and only 20 per cent greater than 70. This 20 per cent, in spite of their higher level of intellectual functioning, will almost certainly encounter difficulties in their lives which will require support and understanding from parents, teachers, therapists, etc. as well as from peers and even employers, to enable them to make the most of their abilities in a world which may not always take kindly to their oddities and eccentricities.

When we first entered the field of autism in the early 1970s, there was little appreciation of the importance of IQ level in the development of autistic children. Indeed, it was believed that intensive educational intervention would 'break through' the barrier of non-communication and ultimately allow the child to develop normally. Two decades later, in the 1990s, this belief seems charmingly naive, and reflects the dearth of knowledge and experience which existed at the time. Since then, the subject of autism has fascinated researchers and clinicians endlessly, and has provided a considerable amount of data which is remakably consistent.

It must be obvious that autistic children with low levels of intelligence will present in a different way from the percentage (albeit small) with higher, even normal intelligence. In general, the most severely autistic children are also likely to be the most severely mentally handicapped. In normally intelligent autistic children, the disability mainly affects verbal skills. This was observed by Rutter who later, when referring to an evaluation of treatment study, commented that, 'The most handicapped children made the least progress in spite of a comparable investment of therapists' time and energy in treatment.'

In the Introduction we referred to the 'often curious skills or islets of ability' which autistic children frequently display. Although the range is circumscribed, there can be many variations. These may include abilities with jigsaws, electrical appliances, knowledge of routes, makes of cars and general feats of memory. Occasionally the skills may be quite exceptional and it is worth mentioning that the proportion of autistic individuals showing savant talents is relatively high. The talents which have been best reported involve artistic, musical and calendrical skills (the ability to work out dates). It is truly extraordinary to encounter such abilities in people who are otherwise severely mentally handicapped.

Problems relating to the diagnosis of autism have been apparent ever since Kanner's time. The situation remains far from satisfactory and is fraught with muddle and confusion. The point-counting approach to diagnosis referred to in Chapter 2 may well have contributed to much of this confusion. We acknowledge that the situation has progressed as researchers have largely moved away from the 'all or nothing' or 'is he or isn't he autistic?' approach. However, this has not filtered down to many clinicians who, through lack of experience of the condition, and therefore a lack of confidence in diagnosis, still adhere to past practice or fail to recognise the existence of autistic features, especially when the condition is less severe. Yet it should be borne in mind that 'classical cases are greatly outnumbered by cases with mixed, impure and partial characteristics' (Shea and Mesibov 1985).

It is our view that a descriptive approach to diagnosis is essential. Only then will the full extent of the autistic continuum be recognised and understood. While acknowledging that more children will be encompassed by less specific diagnostic criteria, autistic spectrum disorders remain comparatively rare. The tendency is for professionals either not to believe that a rare condition could be presented to them, and therefore fail to recognise it, or their own knowledge of the disorder being scanty, any non-classic autistic child is again not recognised because he does not conform to the expectation of what an autistic child 'should be'.

For example, it is particularly easy to overlook autism in a one-to-one situation as many of the more able autistic children respond well to adult attention. Observation of children in a social setting, such as a school or nursery, where their difficulties are more likely to be highlighted among normal functioning peers, is always advisable. However, in the real world, with time and resources at a premium, it is perhaps unrealistic to expect these professionals to constantly update their level of knowledge of one particular disorder among the many they may encounter. Nevertheless, things could be improved.

Many of the recurring diagnostic problems could be alleviated if the training of professionals included greater input on the subject of autism. It is apparent that there is a dearth in the provision of up-to-date information, not only in relation to the training of doctors, but also to that of psychologists and speech and language therapists. Paradoxically, this does not appear to apply as much to the training of teachers of children with special needs. It is an irony that they are usually excluded from the diagnostic process, yet are expected to manage and teach autistic children once they are in an educational setting. Two other groups of professionals whose diagnostic expertise is often undervalued are health visitors and nursery nurses. It is our experience that their wide knowledge of normal child development enables them to pinpoint the deviant patterns seen in young autistic children.

Research Development Units with specialist expertise in autism are very few in number and have difficulty in coping with the referral demand. It is our view that there should be increased use of specialist schools as a district or supra-district resource, which could provide advice and information to any parent of an autistic child, whether or not that child is suitable or eligible for placement in the school. Where this is already happening, there are many obvious benefits. In addition, contacts between schools and research centres provide further opportunities to share and extend knowledge and bridge the gap between academic research and day-to-day routine experience of autistic children. It is as well to keep in mind that, once autism has been diagnosed or identified, the emphasis shifts away from the clinical to an educational setting. Autism is not generally a disorder requiring medical treatment, but one requiring educational management.

In conjunction with this, links with community health and local paediatric departments could form the basis of a comprehensive team approach to diagnosis, provided that the participants were willing to spend time acquiring specialist knowledge and to see children on an *ad hoc* basis. Although, in theory, multi-disciplinary assessment teams already exist in many teaching hospitals, the reality of the situation is nowhere near as utopian as it sounds. It is evident that there is often a scarcity of experience and expertise in many centres where it would be reasonable to expect a high standard of academic thoroughness. In November 1985, The National Autistic Society, increasingly aware of parents' concern and frustration in their pursuit of a diagnosis for their autistic child, issued a report entitled 'What Can The Matter Be?' to draw attention to this serious problem. The results of these referrals, therefore, are often very disappointing in that no diagnosis is made at all, or the presence of autism is strongly denied.

In spite of being critical, we have to acknowledge that there are bound to be problems in diagnosing able autistic children who are very likely to be overlooked by the usual screening procedures. They are not sufficiently handicapped to attract the attention of District Handicap Teams. Instead, they are more likely to be referred to Child Guidance Clinics. In this setting, their behaviour problems are frequently attributed to parental mismanagement, with the result that family therapy is often prescribed. The children's difficulties are seen as the outcome of a breakdown in family dynamics, rather than symptomatic of an underlying disorder. This misinterpretation of the causes of the child's presenting behaviour has brought considerable distress to many parents who feel that they are being blamed undeservedly for their child's problems. Yet they are unable to find an alternative explanation which would make better sense.

When the autism is seen primarily as a 'language disorder with behavioural difficulties', it is likely that there will be a referral to, or back to, a speech and language therapist, with the supposition that remediation of the language problem is all that is required. This 'tidy' explanation is likely to appeal to parents and may also be supported by inexperienced speech and language therapists. They fail to recognise that underlying the behaviour problems are the child's social impairments. It is essential to view the language difficulties in this context in order to promote realistic expectations of outcome.

Sometimes diagnostic problems arise because of the unwillingness of local authorities to acknowledge autism as a viable consideration. In one sense this is reasonable, since the Education Act of 1981, which will be discussed later, is concerned with childrens' individual needs, rather than what are termed 'diagnostic labels'; indeed, autism is no longer a recognised special education category. However, the other side of the coin is the reluctance of some authorities to recognise the disorder because it could lead to demands for additional educational provision which they would have to finance. It is an interesting fact that in areas where there is no provision, or willingness to finance placement in schools elsewhere, autism tends not to exist! Yet, in areas where there is provision, there is no difficulty in filling places. On the contrary, demand exceeds the number of places available.

It is hoped that the establishment of the National Autistic Society's diagnostic centre mentioned earlier, will alleviate most, if not all, of these recurring problems in the recognition and diagnosis of autism.

In the face of all the daunting obstacles, the questions may well be asked, why bother to diagnose at all, especially when the condition is mild, and, who should actually do the diagnosing? As far as the latter is concerned, we think that the professional discipline is unimportant in comparison with the practitioner's experience in the field of autism. The professionals most likely to be involved will include health visitors, speech and language therapists, paediatricians, psychiatrists, clinical and educational psychologists. Obviously, when there are medical factors to consider, the diagnosis is more likely to be the responsibility of a paediatrician who may be hospital or community based. The way in which the diagnosis is presented to parents is of great importance and will be considered in Chapter 6 as part of the subject matter relating to counselling.

The justifications for providing a diagnosis are manifold; parents are entitled to know what is the matter with their own child, and more often than not want to know. Not knowing what is wrong makes them feel vulnerable and insecure, which is more upsetting than many professionals realise. It is by no means unusual for professionals to withhold a diagnosis in the mistaken belief that they are protecting parents from distress. This may in fact reflect their own feelings of inadequacy in coping with the parents' response to bad news, and their own inability to offer support. It is only when their child has been appropriately diagnosed, in a way that makes sense to them, that parents can begin to come to terms with the situation. It is sad to see parents continually seeking consultations, searching for answers, because no one has provided a diagnosis which directly relates to their child's range of difficulties. The provision of a diagnosis ensures that the child's often contradictory problems are not misunderstood. It is very common for the parents of undiagnosed autistic children to feel that they are responsible for their child's 'bad' behaviour. Early diagnosis relieves them of this unnecessary burden of guilt. It is also more likely to promote good management and appropriate treatment, and facilitates access to support groups, services and state allowances. With the correct diagnosis, school placement when the time comes is likely to be more suitable and therefore ultimately more successful. In addition, a meaningful diagnosis enables parents to begin to make plans for the future.

As a rider to these views, we have in mind a particular experience when we were asked to assess a young child who had been seen regularly by a multi-disciplinary team in an assessment centre attached to a childrens' hospital. We were warned not to distress the mother who brought her child to the centre, by mentioning a diagnosis of autism, which we understood the team suspected and wanted verified. It was apparent that the child was indeed autistic. During our conversation, the mother remarked, 'I have been coming here for eighteen months and no one will tell me what is the matter with my child. But I've had a letter from the Housing Department which says that my son is autistic.' This was clearly a well-intentioned endeavour by the team to obtain better housing for the family. The fact that they omitted to share their diagnostic conclusions with the child's mother would seem to be a grievous omission, which led directly to her learning the diagnosis in this unsuitable way.

We are aware that there is an apparent contradiction in our discussion on diagnostic issues. On the one hand we are urging a move away from what we have described as a rigid point counting system, and an all or nothing approach. Yet, on the other hand, we constantly refer to 'autistic children', emphasising the importance of a diagnosis, which in itself suggests that we are guilty of using the very same criteria ourselves! We want to emphasise that we use the term 'autistic' in a *contextual* sense. It follows, therefore, that there is an expectation of a wide diversity of symptoms, features, abilities, intelligence, behaviour, etc. The common denominator will be the underlying social impairments which are on a continuum of severity.   Perhaps if, in relation to autism, the professionals talked of *recognition*, rather than diagnosis, the contradictions would be lessened and misunderstandings would diminish. At the end of the day, call it diagnosis, recognition, or whatever, the professional is confronted with the problem of conveying to the parents the nature of their child's difficulties. The terms, labels, or descriptions used, will depend on the integrity, experience and commonsense of the professional on whom the responsibility falls, for whatever the reason. When the term 'autistic' is used, it is always necessary to provide detailed explanations of what is actually meant. The presence or absence of particular features associated with autism will then be less likely to confuse and mislead parents. Many parents, and even professionals, have been known to express surprise that it is possible to recognise autism with relative ease in a short period of time. It is apparent that anyone with real experience of the condition develops almost a sixth sense and somehow learns to home in on salient details which reveal the nature of the difficulties and make autism an appropriate diagnosis.

It is less likely that there will be much argument over the use of 'autistic' as a term, where the child's difficulties are so apparent that mainstream education would be out of the question. Nevertheless, we feel that it is important not to fudge the existence of a severe mental handicap, by focusing solely on the autism. However, the problem is considerably more complex with children who are only minimally affected, and it is necessary to bear in mind that these minimal features tend to diminish during the middle years of childhood, or even fade into eccentric normality at the very top end of the continuum. This is where the professional's integrity comes in. Are the child's difficulties so mild, that mention of the word 'autism' would generate more problems than it would solve? Even if there is to be no mention of autism, because it would not seem entirely appropriate, it is encumbent upon the professional to clarify the nature of the child's problems, so that parents are not left in any doubt of the long-term implications. This will enable them to ease the way for their child and encourage better understanding and acceptance without emphasising abnormality.

It is a fact that there are children, albeit few in number, who in early childhood display overt autistic features; yet as they develop, sufficient progress is made for the child to cope in a mainstream setting without any extra support. Such difficulties that remain would appear very subtle indeed. A diagnosis of autism should not therefore always imply a 'no hope – doom and gloom' outlook for parents. The situation is by no means as rigid and predetermined as some earlier literature may have suggested.

Chapter 5

Understanding autism: assessing the autistic child

In this chapter we are going to describe different aspects of autism in an attempt to provide a framework for looking at the whole child and evaluating his/her individual difficulties as well as possible abilities and skills. When this approach is used, it is then possible to make sense of this perplexing condition with all its apparent contradictions.

Our previous publication, *Is This Autism?* (Aarons and Gittens 1987), consisting of a checklist and handbook, was designed for the use of professionals to enable them to know what to look at and how to interpret the findings in order to obtain a balanced understanding of the relative skills and deficits of autistic children. It provides a structured framework for assessment and is developmentally based. It is not necessary for parents to use the checklist itself, as it is essentially a clinical tool. However, we will refer to the same key areas of the child's development which form section headings within the checklist. The areas that we look at are as follows:

1 Medical history and early development which will include relevant background information.

2 General observations of the child, relating to appearance, behaviour, and social development.

3 The ability of the child to attend and concentrate.

4 The child's perceptual abilities, primarily in relation to vision and hearing, as well as to other senses.

5 The child's ability to use objects meaningfully, and to play constructively, socially and imaginatively.

6   The child's grasp of concepts which will range from simple matching to more complex levels of understanding.

7   The child's understanding of order or sequence (both visual and auditory). The latter will include the child's interest and response to rhythm and music.

8   The child's understanding and use of speech and language, which will be considered separately in Chapter 7.

9   The child's intellectual capability and, if old enough, his/her attainments in school, which will also be discussed as a separate issue in Chapter 8.

MEDICAL HISTORY AND EARLY DEVELOPMENT

We have already listed some of the medical conditions known to be associated with autism when considering the biological causes. In addition, it is not uncommon to find that autistic children have had a difficult birth history. As well as the febrile episodes which were mentioned in Chapter 4, parents have reported food allergies and other manifestations, many of which remain anecdotal rather than scientific. Yet the majority of autistic children appear to have an uncomplicated start to life and there is nothing of particular significance in records of their early development.

Milestones: sitting, crawling and walking, are more often than not within normal limits. So, in the first year, there may be little evidence of general developmental delay. However, detailed questioning of parents will reveal a number of significant aspects that form a pattern of deviance which will be very familiar to the experienced clinician. Few parents have substantial knowledge of child development, apart from milestones, so that the subtle aspects of their child's behaviour go unnoticed. This is apparent in relation to early communication. Normal infants have been observed from a very young age to engage in a synchronised dialogue with their mothers. The babies' movements are timed to allow a response from her, like a two-way conversation without words. This is the basis for social development and is likely to be absent in babies who are later diagnosed as autistic.

Some parents will describe a baby who does not reach out to be picked up, yet may enjoy physical contact and being cuddled and tickled and, at a later stage, rough and tumble play. A baby described as 'very good', who will lie for hours in his or her pram watching shadows, sunbeams and the movement of leaves. There may be a sustained interest in lights and reflections. Other parents will tell a different story. A baby who screamed incessantly and could not be comforted. Later, as the infant becomes more mobile, an interest in electrical plugs, switches, as well as appliances, may develop. Although normal mobile infants may head for the television set, they are generally easily diverted and are interested in other things. For the autistic infant, the interest may be exclusive and persistent. From an early age the child will learn to work the video, television and stereo, etc., often with great facility, which encourages parents to believe that the child is precocious in development. Sometimes, the infant will spend time watching the washing machine go round and may enjoy feeling the vibrations of electrical appliances. Vacuum cleaners are often a source of great interest. Spinning the wheels of toy cars is another common preoccupation and the young child will resort to these activities when left to his or her own devices. Conventional toys, unless they have wheels to spin, or lights to flash, may be of little interest. As the child develops, so do the patterns of deviance. Despite the normality of early milestones, an overall picture of developmental delay may emerge. Possibly the child who gazed at leaves and shadows, now scrutinises objects from an odd angle while endeavouring to catch reflections or obtain some other visual stimulation.

At this point we must stress that normal infants and young children may engage in many of these activities. However, they do not form an overall persistent pattern that excludes other more meaningful interests.

Many young autistic children do not show particular preference for their parents and are undiscriminating in their responses to people. Others may display what could be described as an almost obsessive attachment to one or other parent. Some maintain indifference to human contact and confine their obsessive attachments to objects, the removal of which will cause them extreme distress which is beyond reason. This is so much at variance with children who are not socially impaired, even if they are mentally handicapped, for whom human beings are of prime importance and interest. It is likely that autistic children are born with the basic knowledge that they are members of the human race either absent or impaired. It is evident that normal babies are predisposed to communicate from birth, and start to make sense of the world within the first few weeks of life. It must be obvious that anything that interferes with these developmental processes will have very serious and far-reaching implications. Without the intrinsic knowledge of the importance of human beings, it is not surprising that autistic children commonly treat people as objects. Those who enjoy physical contact, may use the loving parent rather as a 'cuddling machine' which they will approach to satisfy their own needs. Yet, when the parent wants a cuddle, they are likely to struggle and move away. Similarly, when something is wanted by the child, he or she will use an adult's arm as a tool or, alternatively, will drag the entire body towards the object of his or her desires. This contrasts with the multiplicity of ways in which normal children make their needs known, not least by eye contact, pointing and engaging an adult's interest, as well as by vocalisation. Again, so many of these deviant behaviour patterns would not on their own be of particular significance. It is their coincidence and persistence which are indicative of abnormal development. We cannot emphasise enough, the fact that a normal child continually attracts the attention of his parents for reasons other than basic needs such as obtaining food, and he actively maintains this attention by showing a desire to share his interests. If a child fails to initiate this type of contact and only responds in a limited way to input by the parents, there is reason for concern.

Yet it is easy for parents to ignore or explain away many or all of the signs and symptoms that we have described. It is the child's failure to respond to speech and to develop any himself which causes most concern and leads them to seek professional help, usually during their child's second year. They will often report that the child began to say a few words towards the end of the first year, which were then lost, and had not formed the foundation for further development of language. Other children would only echo or parrot words that were said to them, but again were unable to generate any speech of their own.

While the majority of parents, for whatever reason, do not become concerned about their child's development until well into the seond year, there are some who sense that something is wrong at an earlier stage. Yet looking at their attractive, robust and mobile child, the parents find difficulty in pinpointing exactly what it is that is somehow not quite right. It may be because they recognise that this child is different from an older sibling, or from other children of the same age. To take such a child to a doctor risks a rebuff and the possible label of 'fussy parent'. The course for gaining a meaningful diagnosis is strewn with problems from the outset.

GENERAL OBSERVATIONS – APPEARANCE, MOVEMENT AND BEHAVIOUR

Typically, young autistic children not only look perfectly normal but are positively attractive in appearance. This is one of the so-called myths that seems to be commonly observed and yet defies explanation. Many of these children appear to have an almost ethereal quality, which makes the diagnosis of autism seem all the more unfair and unjust. The attractive appearance is seen in children even where there is a severe degree of mental handicap. Later, however, their attractiveness may seem less striking as, despite maturation, life experiences leave little impression on their features. An empty facial expression, or a far away look, as well as occasional grimacing, are additional characteristics seen in many autistic children.

The avoidance of eye contact has always been associated with autism and until very recently was considered to be of great diagnostic importance. This assumption is very misleading because, although in fact many autistic children *do* avoid eye contact, just as many gaze excessively. Others not only have eye contact, but use it meaningfully, albeit at a rather basic level, for example, looking at an adult for approval.

Many parents of autistic children will have observed their child scrutinising objects at an angle, usually out of the corners of their eyes. Sometimes they will hold an object in order to reflect light, which appears to give them pleasure. Others will lie on the floor for protracted periods while, for example, eyeing a toy train which they repetitively push carefully in and out of a tunnel. It is not unusual to observe young autistic children walking on tiptoe. This may be accompanied by hand flapping and even writhing movements of the fingers which have a sinuous quality. Body twirling is an activity which may be enjoyed, possibly for the sense stimulation it provides.

As we know, the sequence of actions which normal children use to gain the attention of others for the sharing of interests is absent. So often, parents will remark, 'It's as if he is in a world of his own.' Generally, body language is not in evidence. Although many autistic children could be described as hyperactive, just as many are 'lollers'. They will do absolutely nothing unless they are made to participate in some activity. The active autistic children may engage in repetitive but aimless activities, such as running up and down, flicking and twirling objects. More able ones may show more complex repetitive actions. They may line up objects in a set order, or adhere to certain routines, the purpose of which appears to be for maintaining sameness. Verbal autistic children may make factual comments or talk endlessly about topics which are of interest to them, yet be unable to join in reciprocal conversation satisfactorily. Less seriously affected children may show only the subtlest evidence of this characteristic.

In some children, the repetitive activities appear to have a degree of creativity, for example in drawing, pattern making or even building and model making. However, the outcome is stereotyped, although the initial impact of the activity may create a very favourable impression. The range of particular interests and obsessions which autistic children may display is endless. We have already referred to some of them. Other topics of interest we have come across included monsters, makes of cars, timetables, train numbers, Kings and Queens of England, even supermarket bar codes.

In order to gain a greater understanding of an autistic child's pattern of functioning, it is necessary to evaluate evidence of goal-oriented behaviour. If the child is only motivated by food, the prognosis is likely to be less favourable. It is as well to remember that the acquisition of food is a very basic instinct, and the ability of a child to open a freezer and hide away ice-cream for later consumption is not as impressive as it may appear. If, on the other hand, the child shows some resourcefulness in other areas of need and interest, the outlook is better.

It is very usual, but by no means universal, for autistic children to show great distress when exposed to even minor changes which upset their familiar routines. Some children are so bound by their routines that family life is disrupted. They will insist on their parents and brothers and sisters performing certain rituals before they will co-operate even in such simple activities as sitting down for a meal or going shopping. Many autistic children will insist on a certain route being followed and will have a major tantrum if they are taken in a direction which deviates from the one they are familiar with. Yet, paradoxically, more radical changes and new experiences may go unnoticed and these same children will adapt to outings and holidays without any signs of disturbance.

One of the greatest difficulties which even more able autistic children have is the inability to generalise. Although they may know what to do and how to behave in one situation, they are unable to use that experience and adapt it when a new situation arises. There is a pervasive naivety which sets them apart, despite adequate intellectual understanding. For example, a child may have been taught not to make personal comments about Mr Brown's bald head but, when confronted by an obese Mrs Smith, will pass the time of day by drawing attention to her vast size. The inability to generalise extends to all areas of daily life and the degree of difficulty may be disconcerting to the onlooker. An example of this is a boy of twelve who, on a school holiday when told to put shampoo on his hair, a task regularly carried out at home, proceeded to place the bottle on his head.

Awareness of danger is always a problem because, although the autistic child may be taught to avoid a particular danger in a particular situation, he or she cannot anticipate an identical hazard in an unfamiliar setting. As autistic children get older, they may learn strategies for coping with new and unusual situations, especially if they are at the upper end of the autistic continuum. Nevertheless, they will remain vulnerable as it is impossible to teach adaptive skills for all the changes and variations which are part of everyday life.

There have been many attempts to identify sub-groups within the spectrum of autistic disabilities. We have ourselves experience of a few children whose behaviour, while not homogeneous, can be depicted as bizarre in the extreme. For our own use, we have coined the term 'deviant autism' to describe them, although 'Pervasive Developmental Disorder' (a wide-ranging diagnostic grouping in use in the United States) would encompass such children. Typically, there is a developmental history suggesting autism, including delayed language development. Between the ages of four to five years, however, language develops at a rapid rate, and many aspects of autism appear to recede. Hopes may even be raised for an optimistic outcome as many children may make satisfactory academic progress. However, it becomes apparent that, despite this, they develop a pattern of deviant behaviour. Sometimes this is manifested by especially odd and intractable preoccupations which dominate their lives. Other variations of behaviour which encourage us to place children within this group include extreme task avoidance. Despite cajoling or even threats, such a child may spend an entire morning without writing more than a sentence, although he is well capable of considerably greater output. We have encountered children who swear and use verbal abuse, and recently have seen two small boys with autistic histories who display sufficient violence to be excluded from their respective nurseries. These children appear superficially to have an awareness of what goes on in the minds of others. They are particularly adept at knowing how to disturb and annoy people around them, often causing considerable mayhem. It is our view that this behaviour seems to gratify some perverse need in the child, and does not indicate any real awareness of others. As time goes on, the behaviour patterns can become habitual and present difficult management problems. Such children require considerable structure, and may respond well to behaviour modification approaches. We are by no means certain whether it is appropriate to separate these comparatively unusual cases. It may be that they could be included as part of Asperger's Syndrome. (Recently, tentative links have been suggested between Autism and Tourette Syndrome.) Whatever they are called, and however they are grouped, they are extremely difficult to manage both at school and in the home.

The behaviour of more typically autistic children does not appear to be dependent on the level of intellectual functioning, although the ways in which the behaviour is manifested is different. For example, more seriously handicapped children may leap about, yelp and call repeatedly, as well as showing other behaviours which make them conspicuous in the community. More intellectually able children may giggle inappropriately, or repeatedly question and pester adults about inconsequential topics, which again marks them out in society.

This leads us to consider the implications of the social impairments which Lorna Wing has described and which we referred to in Chapter 2. What does this mean in practical terms? The most severely affected children not only fail to respond to language, but shun all physical contact. Attempts to touch and cuddle them are rebuffed and such children really appear to be distressed by the intrusion of people. This extreme isolation is very upsetting for parents as there seems no way in which they can demonstrate affection or even offer comfort when their child is distressed.

Autistic children are often described as 'withdrawn', as though they have taken a decision to remove themselves from society. This represents a misconception of the social difficulties inherent in the condition. The children have *not* withdrawn. In fact, they have not yet learnt to understand and gain pleasure from human contact. Fortunately, as they get older, the majority learn not only to accept physical contact, but even to enjoy it. It may surprise people, who think of autism inevitably in terms of remoteness and isolation, to learn that many autistic children not only like being cuddled, but actively seek out physical contact from which they derive great pleasure. However, as mentioned earlier, many parents, despite the fact that their child initiates such contact, have felt that it was always on the child's terms and was not truly reciprocal.

It is very usual for autistic children to enjoy rough and tumble games, such as tickling, chasing and being swung about. Many autistic children will learn to co-operate in group activities organised by adults. More able individuals will allow themselves to be used by socially normal children in their games and it is possible for them to learn how to behave appropriately in familiar situations. Indeed, at the upper end of the continuum, autistic children and adults may want desperately to participate in social activities but have little or no idea how to go about it. The social skills which normal children acquire without any teaching whatsoever, and the subtleties and nuances which we take completely for granted, are beyond the autistic individual. However great the intellectual capability, lack of social skills is an enormous and wide-ranging handicap which affects every aspect of life. Adolescence is often a difficult time for all young people. For more able autistic teenagers the increasing social complexities may be something of a nightmare. They are aware that they are different, yet are unable to work out what it is they have to do to make themselves socially acceptable. For these young people a programme of social skills training may be very helpful. Such intervention may avert further depletion of confidence and the onset of depression and possibly more difficult behaviour. The pervasive social naivety may lead less inhibited individuals to seek out and ask for sexual contact. Sybil Elgar, known for her pioneering work in the field of autism, has written about these problems. Her paper, together with responses from a number of individuals, may be of interest to parents and others who have to care for older autistic children and adults.

Having examined all aspects of autistic children's development, appearance and behaviour, other areas which we believe to be essential to assess are as follows:

ATTENTION CONTROL

This term describes how well a child is able to concentrate or attend. It is a fundamental necessity for all children and there are developmental stages which range from the extreme distractability of a young baby to the sustained and integrated attention which most 4- to 5-year-olds demonstrate when they enter school (Cooper et al. 1978). In other words, they are ready to learn. Typically the young autistic child is very easily distracted, unless he is focusing on an activity which is of particular interest to him. Those autistic children who develop beyond this level of attention are most likely to make academic progress. Yet it must always be borne in mind that so-called academic progress can often occur in the absence of real understanding, which we will elaborate on later. We cannot stress enough how important it is to consider how well the child attends. So often there is a focus on, say, a lack of speech, without the realisation that the child is failing to attend to what is said to him. Attention is one of the vital underpinnings on which development and learning are based.

SENSORY FUNCTION

This refers to such things as the use of vision, hearing, touch and smell. Visual perception, or the awareness and recognition of visual stimuli, is commonly an area of ability in autistic children. They often show skill in shape matching, jigsaws and formboards. Normal children's abilities in this area progress to the formation of visual concepts; that is, they develop understanding and make sense of what they see. It is always necessary with autistic children to consider whether skill in the area of visual perception is age appropriate or whether it is merely an area of relative ability, meaning better than other aspects of development.

Some psychometric or IQ tests place considerable emphasis on performance skills, which in essence are the abilities which we have just described. This has led more than a few professionals to present a far more optimistic picture of an autistic child's potential than is merited. It is as well to bear in mind that prodigious skill with shape recognition and block design does not indicate abilities which necessarily augur well for future outcome. Additionally, it is not unusual for autistic children to make use of their equally prodigious memories and provide a deceptively favourable impression of their capabilities. Yet there are children who do make progress and who learn visual concepts, albeit at a slower rate and in an incomplete way.

On the auditory or hearing side, autistic children often display particular traits. All too often, they are considered to be deaf, because they do not alert to the human voice and seem quite impervious at times to even loud noises. Such children have even been supplied with hearing aids. Careful observation, however, will reveal that the child hears perfectly well if the sound is of interest to him. For example, the rustle of a sweet paper or opening of a biscuit tin will bring him running from the far end of the house. Some autistic children show extreme distress to auditory stimulii in general, while others demonstrate distress in response to certain sounds, such as a man coughing. They will sometimes attempt to shut out the sounds by putting their hands over their ears. They may also do this when they do not want to heed what is being said to them, or when they want to rid themselves of unwelcome company.

Although some autistic children seem very fleet of foot and physically agile, at least when they are young, it is common for them to ignore the presence of obstructions (human or otherwise). They are likely to walk over someone else's feet with a complete lack of concern for their owner! They may show an equal lack of awareness when a bicycle wheel goes over their own feet. In later childhood and adolescence, even the physically adept children may begin to look awkward; probably because their lack of body language, a symptom of their underlying social impairment, limits the free expression of movement which is part of human communication. It is interesting to speculate why children diagnosed as having Asperger's Syndrome have been described as physically clumsy. We surmise that the clumsiness is in fact the awkwardness which we have described.

Proximal senses – this piece of jargon deals with touching, smelling and feeling. It is very usual for autistic children to sniff, lick or scratch surfaces, themselves, or even other people. These activities are generally associated with the more handicapped children. It is advisable to discourage firmly indiscriminate touching of other people because, although it may be tolerated in a young child, it can become a serious problem with older children and adolescents. It is obviously easier to establish patterns of acceptable behaviour in small, physically manageable children. Another characteristic of some autistic children is a lack of awareness of pain, heat and cold. They are less likely than normal peers to be able to locate and express the source of discomfort.

SYMBOLIC UNDERSTANDING

This means the understanding a child displays in relation to objects and their use, which does not involve language. In other words, we are looking at the quantity and quality of a child's play. The typical play activities, if they exist, of many young autistic children will consist of lining up cars and spinning wheels and other objects, looking or flicking through books and completing jigsaws. There is often a lot of aimless running about, and social play is confined to chasing and rough and tumble pursuits. Swinging, and even lying upside down or in odd positions, can be favoured pastimes. Parents will often report that their autistic child's greatest enjoyment, it would seem in lieu of play, is watching videos and television. Usually there are particular favourites which will be selected time and again.

By the age of 1 year, a normal child recognises familiar objects in his surroundings, such as his cup or bottle, brush or coat. Later, at about 18 months, when his understanding has developed further, he will realise that small sized objects represent the normal sized ones which are familiar to him. At about this time, play with large dolls and toys will be in evidence and the child will begin to demonstrate simple play routines, such as putting a doll to bed, feeding and washing it. From about 2½ years of age a child will begin to enjoy play with miniatures – dolls house-sized people and objects. The play routines will become more complex, and imagination and creativity in the play will become more evident. Many children are less interested in doll play, but will demonstrate creativity and imagination with constructional toys, for example, producing a wide and varied range of vehicles, buildings or roads. The normal child develops further into a social and friendly being who seeks out and enjoys the company of other children. Generally, by the age of 3 years, the child has learnt to take turns to a greater or lesser extent, and to join with his peers in group play and activities from which he derives a great deal of pleasure. In the case history section at the end of the book, we refer to the Lowe and Costello 'Symbolic Play Test'; this consists of a number of simple play scenarios utilising miniature dolls and objects. These scenarios range from feeding, brushing a doll's hair, laying a table, to lining up and loading a tractor and trailer. However, this test has limitations since even severely handicapped autistic children may get a full score, meaning that they can demonstrate appropriate use of all the miniature objects, yet in real life it is clearly obvious that they fail to play imaginatively and creatively.

The essence of developing symbolic understanding in relation to play is variety, inventiveness and imagination. These qualities highlight the characteristics of normal play, contrasted with the play often shown by even more able autistic children. The latter group may indeed play, but there will be a reiteration of certain themes particular to the child's interests. For instance, a child may repeatedly dress and undress dolls, set out meals and feed them. Some children may talk to and for their dolls. Casual or 'once off' observation of such a child's play may result in autism being excluded as a possible diagnosis. Those with experience of the condition will, however, recognise the limitations of the play which, though more complex, is repetitive and fails to lead anywhere. Sometimes autistic children with particular interests can, to some extent, manipulate and develop them and even display some apparent imagination, which again may confuse an inexperienced observer. The interests are likely to be circumscribed and idiosyncratic. For example, one child known to us who was obsessed with vacuum cleaners could not only use them, but he could draw them, model them in plasticine and also pretend to plug them into imaginary electric sockets.

Professor John Morton of the Medical Research Council Cognitive Development Unit, in an article entitled 'The Origins of Autism', has highlighted the essentials of pretend play.

> Not all play is pretend play. Take for example, the case of a child who plays with a toy saucepan on a toy stove, making the kind of movements, for example stirring and shaking, that mother makes on the real stove. This may be merely functional play, a re-enacted memory. However, if the child sniffs and says that there is bacon frying and varies the play according to the dish, then this is pretend.

By the age of 3½ to 4 years, most children seek out and enjoy the company of others. Many professionals working with autistic children, even the high flyers, are astounded when observing normal children, by the richness of their sociability and their in-built capacity to make friends. Somehow, subtle social rules are used and understood without adult intervention. Children with more specific language difficulties may also display impoverished play and sociability, but this usually reflects immaturity rather than the patterns of deviance typical of autistic children. It must be borne in mind that poor play by itself does not indicate autism. It is the coincidence of many behavioural aspects which makes such a diagnosis appropriate.

Yet paradoxically, as autistic children progress towards middle childhood, they may develop a real desire for friends and play opportunities. Fortunately, there are socially normal children who are willing to involve an autistic child in their games and activities, sometimes as a 'baby' or a 'patient' when playing mothers and fathers, or doctors and nurses. Chasing games allow greater scope for drawing in autistic children, although games with subtle rules may prove to be beyond them. Board games, however, do offer scope for more able autistic children as there is a predictability about the way in which they are played and, in addition, a better than average memory may promote success. Cards, chess and draughts are likely to be favoured. Although able autistic children may refer to wanting or having friends, it is inevitable that their concept of friendship is essentially limited; their social impairments, however mild, are an obstruction which will set them apart from the normal population. This is particularly poignant when autistic children express their deep-felt need for friends yet are unable to comprehend why they are unable to acquire them.

CONCEPT FORMATION

This term is used to describe the development of a child's understanding of the world about him. It evolves out of the perceptual processes which we described earlier. Autistic children often display skills and abilities which are either on a par or in advance of their chronological age. It is natural to assume that these skills and abilities would be accompanied by a corresponding level of understanding. Yet this is not the case. Autistic children appear to be able to learn in the absence of understanding, so that the apparent knowledge they have cannot be utilised and extended as would be expected with a normal child. Lorna Wing's comparison of this phenomenon with 'tower blocks in a desert', is a meaningful visual image. It describes well the lack of connections between what is known, and explains the contradictory character of autistic children's learning. As we have already mentioned, the assumption is that these tower blocks, or 'islets of ability' as they are sometimes called, reflect the true level of the child's functioning. It would seem reasonable, therefore, to search for ways to 'unlock' or 'break through' to all other areas of development where, it is assumed, latent ability lies dormant. Sadly, this is not so. The remarkable thing is that very low functioning individuals *can* possess skills and abilities which are not only normal, but may even amount to a gift. In his book *Extraordinary People*, Darold Treffert describes individuals who, though very severely mentally handicapped, can nevertheless show amazing and seemingly inexplicable feats of apparent intellectual prowess, which defy belief. The 'Savant Syndrome' which he describes is of course very rare, but awareness of this condition may enable parents of autistic children with islets of ability to see the abilities in perspective.

Our method of assessing concept development in children with autistic features includes, at the basic level, matching colours, shapes and objects. These tasks require only minimal understanding, but as they increase in complexity towards sorting and classification skills, autistic children commonly run into difficulties. Even when they have adequate intelligence, adequate language and know the facts, they fail to 'cotton on' and see the obvious. An example of this was the inability of a group of three verbal and bright autistic children to appreciate the link between cold drinks and the use of a refrigerator. Despite the fact that they were familiar with fridges, both at home and in school, they were quite unable to respond appropriately to the question, 'Where will we put these drinks to keep them nice and cold?'

It is also necessary to ascertain whether a child has developed an understanding of size, for example, big and small, long and short, fat and thin. Does the child appreciate same and different? Is he aware of quantities, for example, more or less, big, bigger, biggest? Does he understand the position of himself and objects in space, for example, in, on, under, and at a later stage, near, behind, in front of, left and right, etc.?

The sum total of the child's development of understanding the ways of the world can be coined in the current idiom 'street wise'. Autistic children do not have this capability, even when they are intellectually able. They remain naive and unknowing and are vulnerable, despite sensitive and adequate care, input and support throughout their years of education.

SEQUENCING AND RHYTHMIC CAPABILITIES

The ability to understand the passing of time and the sequence of events is a skill which has important implications. Once again, more able autistic children will be able to learn how to sequence colours or shapes in order, but may not be able to use this facility to arrange pictures in sequence to form a meaningful story, especially if the story involves the attribution of states of mind. It is possible that, once shown the correct order, an autistic child may learn the sequence and may even accompany this with an appropriate commentary. However, this should be regarded with some caution, as it is likely to be a feat of memory rather than evidence of true understanding. The commentary used by the child may simply echo that used by whoever presented the task.

Eventually, many autistic children learn to appreciate the passing of time. Their anxieties are reduced as they gain understanding and life generally becomes more predictable for them. They remember past events and look forward to the future, albeit at a simple level. Gaining this understanding can have a positive effect on management, as the child learns not to expect immediate gratification, but instead gains some pleasure from anticipation.

Awareness and enjoyment of rhythm and music is common in the autistic population, and often autistic children show good musical ability. Music therapy may have a very useful place in their education, especially when spoken language is absent. The child is encouraged to interact and initiate musically with the therapist. It must not be assumed that music therapy will be a panacea, but it can provide not only enjoyment, but the beginnings of a dialogue which may accelerate the child's rate of development.

Chapter 6

Practical considerations – management and counselling

Much has been written about the management of autistic children and the difficulties parents encounter. At the outset, it is perhaps necessary to make the point that what one set of parents will regard as a major problem, another set of parents will cope with and not regard as a problem at all. For example, one parent who related how easy it was to manage her autistic 3-year-old, reported (among a prodigious list of her son's idiosyncracies) that she and her husband were perfectly happy for their child to keep them company every evening until they all went to bed at around midnight. Clearly her priorities were different from those of many others, who would willingly dispatch their offspring to bed at midday! It is common for autistic children to require very little sleep and many parents report that nights are interrupted and the household disturbed for years on end. It is not unknown for such parents to reach the end of their tether and, in desperation, resort to locking their autistic child in his bedroom. Although this measure may invoke shock/horror reactions, it is entirely understandable in the context of a child wandering around the house, not only waking everyone up, but possibly harming himself and not least wreaking havoc in his wake.

Because of the idiosyncratic nature of autism, other problems requiring careful management may occur. Some relate to the child's insistence on repeating particular activities, such as opening and shutting doors, watching a particular video, listening to a particular record, or persistent and meaningless questioning over and over again. One of the advantages of joining a parent support group, is that problems can be aired and management techniques shared, which is sometimes a lifeline for fraught families. Many parents have shown great ingenuity in solving what appear to be very daunting problems, sometimes with the injection of humour which eases the burden.

Articles and books on the management of children with behaviour problems may be invaluable. *Helping Your Handicapped Child* by Janet Carr, which is a Penguin Handbook, is an example. An article reprinted in the National Autistic Society journal *Communication*, by Caroline Seheult, provides some particularly useful and constructive ideas in relation to behaviour or conditioning therapy for such children which can be carried out by parents. (*Communication* is a quarterly journal published by the National Autistic Society for both professionals and parents. It provides very readable and informative articles which by no means necessarily reflect the views of the Society.) The National Autistic Society has published a number of booklets that provide advice on problems more specific to autistic children, such as obsessive and ritualistic behaviours.

The range of management problems does appear to have a certain predictability and many of them will be similar to those encountered among mentally handicapped children. Sometimes progress with toilet training will be particularly slow; some children will only use a particular toilet. Others become either obsessed with, or terrified of, the flush. Dressing and self-care skills may be well within a child's capability, yet he will refuse to co-operate; hands adept for chosen activities become floppy and useless when it comes to putting on socks and doing up buttons. Parents will go on dressing an older autistic child, sometimes in desperation, in order to get him to school on time.

Eating habits and likes and dislikes are often extreme. Children may eat only a very limited range of foods or insist on eating and drinking only from certain plates and cups. Some children are resolute in their refusal to eat sensibly and consequently have a waif-like appearance while existing apparently on air. Others may be obese on a diet which consists exclusively of burgers and chips. A sustained programme of persuasion, and even coercion, to accept an increasing range of different foods has, in our experience, been very successful. For parents, who for some time have been locked into a particular pattern of food provision, this may be impossible to carry out, and is therefore best implemented as part of a nursery/school programme. Not only do the children then have a wider diet in school, but there is frequently a carry over into home. With a better diet, the appearance of the children may improve quite dramatically and their behaviour becomes less 'cranky'.

Parents of normal children may well have encountered similar problems. With autistic children the complete lack of amenability and their intractability are of diagnostic significance when viewed in conjunction with other behavioural features. Some parents feel that their autistic child's anti-social table manners and unpredictable behaviour precludes the possibility of eating out as a family. Even modest excursions to the local McDonald's, let alone to grander establishments, are so fraught with potential embarrassment that they are hardly worth contemplating. A particular family known to us found a solution to this problem which was both simple and effective, as well as unstressful. They decided not to inflict their son on the local community, nor on people whose enjoyment of gastronomic delights would be seriously marred by his presence. They hit upon the idea of utilising the eating facilities of motorway service stations for training purposes. Their fellow diners, an anonymous population in transit, paid little heed to their son's outbursts, and while the family became acquainted with the country's motorways, the autistic child's social eating habits improved dramatically. The family is now able to eat anywhere with enjoyment and confidence.

Some autistic children, usually those who are more handicapped, have the habit of 'pica', which means that they will eat inedible substances, such as buttons, Blu-Tack, worms, sand, decaying leaves. Such children have to be watched very carefully as, within a matter of a split second, the child may make a grab for whatever he has a predilection for and is well on the way to swallowing it before the adult has even realised what is happening.

We have lost count of the parents who relate horror stories about their autistic offspring and shopping expeditions. Many of our major supermarkets have witnessed sensational tantrums as an autistic child gives vent to his particular dislike of shopping procedures – not least checkout queues. Many parents have been upset by the attitude of other shoppers who, belied by the child's normal appearance, comment adversely about lack of discipline. More resilient parents will not alter their shopping habits and will cope with trolley and child while informing the critics about the nature of autism! Additionally, a child's lack of awareness of danger will compound the difficulties associated with even the simplest trip outside the home. One parent solved the problem of a child refusing to have his hand held in the street by introducing a benign form of handcuffs! This consists of a webbing strip with Velcro fastenings which can be circled round both the child's and the adult's wrists. It allows the child to feel free, while being constrained from running off; a simple and effective device, which is available from Mothercare. The majority of parents of autistic children are likely to alter their lives in order to avoid not only shopping expeditions, but other outings too. Sadly, some parents are so stressed by the behaviour of their young autistic child while they are outside the home that their own lives become increasingly restricted, which may have serious repercussions on partners and other children in the family.

We have already mentioned that some autistic children are afraid of lavatories flushing. In addition, such children may become fearful of a wide assortment of innocuous things which may range from the more rational, for example, dogs, to the irrational, such as someone coughing. Some fears are transient, only to be replaced by new ones, whilst others are longer lasting. Masturbation in public is often a problem with autistic children and can cause parents a great deal of embarrassment. Sometimes common sense strategies can prevent the worst excesses of the habit. For example, dressing children in trousers that are reasonably tight fitting around the waist and without elastic, with the addition of braces, can deter the child from constantly pulling down or putting his hands down his trousers!

It is important to emphasise the fact that no two autistic children are alike. Each presents in an individual way which reflects his or her own personality, family background and experiences. Their individuality exists in exactly the same way as in the normal population. We need to emphasise this, as so often professionals fail to recognise autism because the child in front of them is very different from the autistic child they saw once upon a time. To those with experience, the autistic strands will be evident, despite the multiplicity of permutations that are possible.

HELP AND ADVICE

Counselling is a word which has passed into common use and is applied not only to survivors of disasters, and the bereaved, but to those with less dramatic or acute problems, the effects of which may be no less devastating for some people. There is something particularly poignant about discovering that you are the parent of an autistic child. As we have already mentioned, typically autistic children are normal and attractive looking. Developmental milestones are often within normal limits and the child may even display precocious ability in particular areas. Often, for as long as two years or more, the parents will have believed that their somewhat odd or puzzling child was normal, if not bright, and at worst appeared to be delayed in acquiring language. To then learn that the child has an intractable and lifelong handicap is likely to come as a terrible blow. Obviously we do not want to minimise the trauma for parents learning that their newborn baby has a serious handicap, such as Down's Syndrome, which also has lifelong implications. However, right from the start their expectations are of necessity defined by their awareness of the handicap. Conversely, the parents of the child later diagnosed as autistic, have expectations of normality. To then discover that the child they believed to be perfect is seriously handicapped, may be, as one parent put it, 'like being told you have cancer'.

Parents in this situation will often deny the diagnosis very vigorously, or may embark on a series of consultations with professionals of a variety of disciplines, as well as those promising miraculous cures, in attempts to prove the diagnosis wrong and to find out 'what is *really* the matter'. In fact they want to be told that their child is normal and will 'grow out of it', which is most understandable. Perhaps this is a reason why some parents are attracted to unsubstantiated treatment programmes such as holding therapy. It offers hope, and it must be acknowledged that there are parents who would choose to live in an unreal world where assurances of a cure are provided, despite all evidence to the contrary. This may reflect a failure on the part of professionals to provide the right quality of support for parents. It requires considerable skill to be realistic, yet keep alive a positive and hopeful state of mind in parents so that they feel that they can play an active part in developing their child's full potential. Yet we have been surprised by the strength of feeling in parents who assert that they would rather live with false hopes of a cure for the condition of autism, than accept what we would call a realistic appraisal of the situation. We would argue that sooner or later these parents are likely to feel extremely angry and disappointed when their hopes are not fulfilled, and may well blame teachers and therapists for not putting in enough effort into making their child better. We have the impression that such situations are more likely to arise where there is underlying depression in one or both parents or where the marriage is under stress; a handicapped child is then the final straw.

Coming to terms with the diagnosis is, in effect, coming to terms with the loss of a child through bereavement, and learning to contemplate a future for their child and themselves which is different from their previous expectations. This process, just as with bereavement, can take some considerable time and will be as individual as the people undergoing the experience. We understand the trauma parents may feel when their child who, five minutes earlier, they had regarded as normal with seemingly minor problems, is now 'autistic'. One parent vividly expressed her feelings after hearing the diagnosis: 'I looked at her and all I could feel was, you poor thing, you are an autistic child.' It was as if the child she had known was no longer there and the little girl became the personification of a label. Fortunately, in our experience, these negative feelings pass with time and parents are able to see that, despite the autism, their child is still the same. It is only their own perceptions or awareness that has altered. All autistic children have aspects of normality and these can be enjoyed. They do develop and, just as with normal children, they will give both pleasure and pain to their parents.

We were motivated to write this book to provide information and answers to the many questions that parents asked at this particularly difficult time. There is so little knowledge of autism among professionals that anything we could provide to prevent misinformation would be of value. It is our view that the more knowledge parents have, the more they will be able to make informed decisions relating to their child's needs. The parents' questions covered all areas, from practicalities of daily living . . . 'What can we actually do to help?' . . . to 'What will happen when we are gone?'. We recognise that although many parents do require skilled counselling from people with experience of autism, there are too few individuals who are able to offer this help. It is often a matter of luck or chance that some parents are well supported and advised, while others flounder for years on end without receiving an appropriate diagnosis, let alone appropriate advice and support.

For this reason, these very general guidelines might be useful. However, we have some reservations about giving specific advice, because it might seem as if we are saying, 'Do this and the problem will be solved'. It is not as simple as this in practice. Autistic children are so variable that it is almost impossible to generalise about what may or may not be appropriate, or to predict what will or will not work with individual children. The last thing we want to do is promote the idea of failure when one or all of our suggestions do not work for a particular child. As often as not, lateral thinking and trial and error produce just as good solutions for alleviating problems, just as the passing of time allows a child to grow out of a particularly difficult phase and become easier to manage. Generally, autistic children do become more amenable once past infancy. This is not to say that the troubles are over, but the most exhausting problems, relating to sleeping, eating, temper tantrums, etc. do tend to recede and life becomes calmer. First of all, be consistent with your child. In other words, do not keep changing the goal posts. Decide on a set of rules and try to stick to them, so that the child knows where he is. It is important to establish priorities. Go for the things that are essential and be prepared to waive the less important.

Remember that until a child can attend to a task or activity for at least a few minutes at a time, he will not be ready to benefit from attempts at teaching. It may be more helpful for parents to focus on helping their child to attend as an end in itself, rather than attempting to teach new skills. As the child's attention span increases, so will the range of relevant goals. For example, rather than trying to get a distractible child to name pictures in a book, aim to persuade him to sit down and share looking and listening activities, and inhibit page flipping and fixations on details such as words or numbers on a page which may be meaningless.

Be aware of the child's developmental level and not necessarily his chronological age, so that only developmentally appropriate skills are taught, with simple and immediate rewards for success. It may be possible to use the child's repetitive activities (such as twiddling, which he enjoys doing) as a reward, when he has done something that you want him to do. Physical punishment is not generally appropriate. The exception may be in an extreme or life-threatening situation such as when a child dashes into the road, or climbs on to a high ledge. In such situations, any punishment must immediately follow the deed, so that an association is made, even if the danger is not understood.

It is not helpful to regard the behaviour of autistic children in terms of 'being naughty'. The concepts of naughtiness and goodness may be well beyond the child's level of understanding.

A straightforward rule-based approach is likely to be more effective than long involved explanations. Therefore, 'No, don't do that', is sufficient and will cause less confusion. If changes are to be made, do not try to do everything at once. Deal with one issue at a time.

If your child is not yet in a nursery or playgroup, then take steps to ensure that a suitable placement is found at the earliest opportunity. It is likely that if a child is known to have special needs, priority will be given. We feel that, unless the child's difficulties are very mild indeed, parents should be open about their child's problems and not attempt to conceal them from the playgroup or nursery. Teachers and playgroup leaders are generally prepared to give a young child a chance and will do their best for him. However, if they feel that a child has been presented as normal when the parent is aware of substantial difficulties, they are less likely to feel sympathetic to the situation.

A possible disadvantage of an early diagnosis of autism (say when a child is between 2 to 3 years of age) is the fact that many parents then feel that their child must enter a special school setting immediately, if he is to make maximum progress. We want to stress that this is by no means the best course of action as it would mean depriving the child of opportunities to mix with normal children, and to learn from them. Young autistic children, just like any others, need time to mature and gain skills and social experience which will underpin their future learning in school.

It is important to be vigilant in not confusing the child with well-meaning but misguided untruths. For example, a little autistic girl knew that she must not touch hot things. Her parents, wishing to dissuade her from constantly fiddling with the video recorder, told her that it too was hot. This was a short-term ploy which was very unhelpful as it confused her understanding of the nature of heat. It would have been far better to have simply said, consistently, 'No, don't touch', and to have meant it.

The underlying principle in the management of autistic children, regardless of their developmental level, is the building of bridges for understanding. Bearing in mind that autistic children lack the ability to make sense of the world about them, it follows that efforts to make things meaningful to them is a worthwhile endeavour.

Some parents are fortunate enough to live in an area where a Portage scheme is in operation. This service provides help and advice on a domiciliary basis for children with developmental difficulties. Parents are shown how to play an active part in facilitating progress in small steps towards relevant goals. Young autistic children may gain much benefit from the Portage approach, and we would advise parents who are given the opportunity to participate, to take advantage of the scheme. In some areas toy libraries exist and parents of autistic children may find them a useful resource. Similarly, play schemes for handicapped children may be available and are generally well organised. Again, autistic children can derive much benefit by participating. A contact address is listed at the back of the book (see Appendix 2, pp. 119–21).

Perhaps one of the worst scenarios is when the autistic features are misunderstood by well-meaning, but ill-informed, professionals who interpret the child's difficulties as symptomatic of the parents' mismanagement and poor parenting skills. This so often feeds on the guilt that many parents of handicapped children appear to suffer, and delays more constructive approaches and attitudes to the problems that the family is experiencing. We feel that it is difficult enough to have to cope with a handicapped child, without being blamed even indirectly for causing it. Our invariable practice is, when making a diagnosis of autism, to emphasise to parents that they have *not* caused the condition, which is not to say that some aspects of their management of the child could not be improved upon. It is evident that the most stable, happy and well-organised families would, if an autistic child was placed in their midst, be likely to succumb to exactly the same pressures which are so familiar to us and others working in the field.

In some families, life revolves around the autistic member. Brothers and sisters are often required to put up with constant intrusions into all aspects of their lives. Sometimes they feel that they cannot entertain friends at home because of embarrassment caused by their autistic sibling. Sometimes family outings do not happen because of problems associated with both taking and leaving the autistic child. In one family, not only had outings ceased, but the parents felt such deep shame at having a handicapped child that the mother became almost reclusive in an attempt to conceal the child from public gaze. The child in question is, in fact, a bright little girl, a delight to look at, and one who is able to benefit from social experiences.

In some families there is a tendency for the normal children to feel or take on more responsibility for their autistic brother or sister than is perhaps either appropriate or necessary. This may be nurtured by the parents, who perhaps cherish the notion of family togetherness. However, when this happened in one particular family, a normal brother who had had to devote too much of his life to two younger autistic brothers, took himself off to the other side of the world at the earliest opportunity. We felt not a little admiration for a mother who took a very positive stance in relation to her daughter who, she vowed, would never be made to feel responsible for her very handicapped, older, autistic brother. The National Autistic Society is concerned about the possible adverse effects on siblings of having an autistic child in the family. A small group meeting for interested brothers and sisters was held in 1989, and the outcome was that such meetings were beneficial, but would be better organised on a regular and regional basis. Patricia Howlin, one of the organisers of this group, has written a paper on this subject (Howlin 1989).

While coping with the autistic child in the family, the needs of the normal children must be attended to. However, we are very aware that it is not simply a matter of forgetting about these needs, but rather the logistics of finding time and energy to attend to them more than minimally. Even if there are no other children, the relationship between partners may be severely stressed for the same reasons. Evenings that are taken up by an autistic child do little to cement relationships. Although it may be comparatively easy to find babysitters for normal children, many parents are reluctant to impose their autistic offspring on someone outside the family, and even sometimes within it.

Respite care, which consists of placement in a residential home for weekends and holiday periods, etc., sometimes on a regular basis, is welcomed with relief by some parents. These homes may be in the voluntary sector, but some are provided by local authorities. Other organisations arrange respite care on an individual family basis, so that a difficult child can be 'adopted' for odd days or weekends to give his hard-pressed family a break. The address of Contact-a-Family is listed in Appendix 2 (see pp. 119–21). They may be able to put parents in touch with local schemes of this kind. Sometimes, when respite care is offered to parents under stress, it is rejected; however ghastly the home circumstances may be, such a suggestion confirms feelings of guilt and anxiety. This is understandable but very unproductive. Usually, after counselling, parents can see the advantages of time away from their autistic child and learn not only to accept the offer, but take positive steps to use the time beneficially. Sometimes acceptance of respite care saves the rest of the family from falling apart, while the autistic child suffers no ill effects whatsoever.

Boarding schools specifically for autistic children are few in number, but other suitable alternatives may be available for placement. Sometimes families cope well until later childhood or early adolescence, when the autistic child's behaviour, coupled with his or her ever-increasing size, causes mayhem. The same feelings of guilt and inadequacy may also arise when a boarding placement is suggested. Yet the separation can promote an improvement in behaviour which in itself establishes a better climate within the family.

However, there is no right or wrong way for parents and siblings to cope. Each family must work out its own salvation, hopefully with care and support from knowledgeable professionals. Perhaps by providing a few examples of the ways in which families have responded to the presence of an autistic child in their midst, others will see their own circumstances reflected, which may enable them to seek help in order to make beneficial changes.

Parents of autistic children may not be aware that they may qualify for an attendance allowance from the Department of Social Security. Although obtaining it may involve perseverance and fortitude, the extra money may facilitate changes which will benefit the whole family.

As a postscript, having given this rather gloomy picture of possible family difficulties, we want to emphasise that some autistic children are not at all difficult to live with and show their problems in more subtle ways.

Chapter 7

Speech and language: communication development in autistic children

There are certain characteristics relating to speech and language development which are peculiar to autistic children. Firstly, delay in its acquisition is especially common (and this delay has to be considered in relation to the child's overall developmental level). Uta Frith, in *Autism: Explaining the Enigma,* points out that delays in language acquisition may or may not indicate a fundamental language disorder. Normal children acquire language because of a strong and innate desire to communicate. It follows that if the motivation to communicate is impaired, as it is with autistic children, then this will be a contributing factor to the delayed acquisition. Indeed, this is often the reason why children, later diagnosed as autistic, are referred in the first place and why speech and language therapists are so often the first professionals to become involved. Parents are likely to report that at the latter end of the first year, the child began to acquire speech but then seemed to lose it. When speech eventually appears, there is a pattern of deviance which differs from that shown by children with more specific language difficulties. Essentially the problems centre around the *use* of language. The child may acquire adequate linguistic structures to communicate and indeed may do relatively well in standardised language assessments, but fails to engage successfully in interactive communication.

We are now beginning to examine this 'communicative intent' in a practical way. We use a simple assessment called 'A Pragmatic Profile' (Dewart and Summers 1988). Its aim is to build up a picture of how a young child attempts to use language to make his needs and interests known and, in terms of age and abilities, how effective these strategies are. This profile must be evaluated in relation to the child's level of overall development. It is not unusual for the speech and language problems of autistic children to be described as a 'semantic-pragmatic disorder', and this label has been the cause of some debate at the time of writing. Those who have little or no experience of autism, particularly in its mildest form where there are few classic features, may view the language peculiarities of verbal autistic children as a separate disorder. It is our view that a focus solely on language and linguistic features, without regard to the child's mode of being, is inadequate and simplistic. Knowledge of the child's developmental history and an evaluation of his interests, play, relationships, etc., are essential if the true nature of the difficulties is to be understood. In other words, the presence of autism, however mild or subtle, must be recognised. It is then that these children make sense. The medical model notion of a disorder has generated considerable muddle among speech and language therapists and other professionals and has prevented them from appreciating the underlying aetiology which is crucial to expectations of outcome. The debate could be resolved by the replacement of the word 'disorder' with 'difficulties', which would encourage clinicians to use the term descriptively rather than diagnostically.

The following list will highlight the deviant aspects of speech and language as it develops in autistic children:

1 The child does not alert to the human voice, despite normal hearing, but may be aware of other sounds that interest him. These may be idiosyncratic, such as plumbing noises, or relate to food, such as a biscuit tin being opened.

2 Comprehension is poor, or even non-existent, and the autistic child shows little interest in communicating, except perhaps for his own needs and particular idiosyncratic interests. Deceptively, the poor comprehension is often masked by superficially fluent expressive speech. (See no. 11.)

3 There is little or no attempt to give messages with eyes or gesture and mime. This will include pointing out objects of interest.

4 The child does not engage an adult's attention to share an interest. This can be seen in normal children, even before their first birthday.

5 A large naming vocabulary may be acquired, which means that the child can successfully label everyday objects.

6 Immediate echolalia is particularly common; the child will repeat all or part of what is said to him.

7 The autistic child somehow learns phrases, sentences, even sophisticated chunks of language, which he is able to reproduce often in the appropriate context. For example, a bright autistic child in a language unit was able to reprimand a disruptive child in the group, using verbatim his teacher's words: 'You'll have to leave the room if you can't sit still and listen.'

8 Often television jingles are retained and repeated, as are songs, nursery rhymes, etc.

9 Questions present particular problems. The child fails to acknowledge them in conversation, but may produce a reply if suitably 'cued in'. It is as if certain triggers elicit appropriate responses and associations.

10 There is often particular difficulty in using those parts of speech which change their meaning, for example, the pronouns 'I' and 'you'. This also applies to the use of prepositions, 'in', 'on', 'under', 'next to', etc. These may be understood in a controlled situation, but not in a wider context.

11 The verbal autistic child appears to be able to say more than he can understand. Poor comprehension may be masked by seemingly appropriate responses. Phrases such as, 'I can't remember', may in fact mean, 'I haven't understood what you are saying.' Some children can display considerable anxiety and panic when they are spoken to in a way which does not immediately make sense to them. In other words, if what they hear does not fit in to their repertoire of understanding, they are at a loss to know what is expected of them. Hence the panic.

12 Interactive communication skills are very poor which means that the child cannot participate normally in a conversation.

13 Turn taking and the accompanying strategies, such as nodding and appropriate body language, are absent or impaired.

14 There are rarely problems relating to the clarity of speech, but pitch and intonation may be odd.

15 The child with speech may talk *at* people, often about his particular interests which may range from monsters to railway timetables. The listener is not taken into account.

16 The child's understanding is literal. He fails to pick up inferences, and information which is presented indirectly. An example of this, is a child who, when asked by his teacher if he could find his mid-morning milk, looked in the appropriate place, answered 'yes', but made no attempt to take a bottle as was expected.

17 The child's use of language is concrete and shows little flexibility.

18 Humour, if present, is likely to be confined to slapstick or puns and wordplay.

It will be apparent from the list that what is distinctive about the language of autistic children is that it reflects the cognitive and social impairments which we described earlier. Non-autistic children with a specific language disorder will certainly show difficulties with the understanding as well as the expression of language but, although probably immature, their social development is not deviant. They are likely to find alternative means of expressing themselves, and are capable of engaging in the sequence of attracting attention, and sharing their *varied* interests. To clarify the differences between high level autism (or so-called Semantic–Pragmatic Disorder) and true language delay/disorder, we have included a chart for easy reference (see pp. 64–5). Descriptions of semantic–pragmatic disorder in the literature are often confusing and contradictory. The authors often seem more familiar with research literature than long term, day to day contact with children. There also appears to be a concern for defining boundaries between disorders for research purposes (the medical model approach).

Bishop (1989) recommended using the term 'specific semantic-pragmatic disorder' for:

> children who are not autistic but who initially present with a picture of language delay and receptive language impairment, and who then learn to speak clearly and in complex sentences, with semantic and pragmatic abnormalities becoming increasingly obvious as their verbal proficiency increases . . . the

pattern of verbal deficits looks more distinctive as they grow older.

(Some speech and language therapists have used the term in relation to language difficulties which do not conform to the pattern of deviance described by Bishop. This has compounded the confusion and reflects, perhaps, an excess of enthusiasm for the term rather than clinical diligence.)

Although Bishop provides a very thorough overview of the autism/semantic–pragmatic debate, her conclusions seem to suggest that we should adhere to 'conventional diagnostic criteria for autism'. This, presumably, means a point counting 'Is he/isn't he autistic' approach of the kind that Kanner suggested fifty years ago.

This approach is at odds with developments in current research in the field of autism, where it is recognised as essential to look at all aspects of the child, in a variety of settings (as well as a developmental history) when making a diagnosis. To disregard these developments to validate the existence of a separate language disorder is a dubious way of clarifying issues. What does Bishop mean by 'not autistic'? Certainly, these children may not be classically autistic. However, to regard children displaying such communication deficiencies as merely language disordered is too simplistic.

Unless the language peculiarities are regarded as merely the tip of the iceberg the child's real underlying difficulties will not be recognised. Subsequent focus of therapy on linguistic aspects will be neither helpful nor appropriate. We cannot emphasise enough that children displaying this pattern of language development have an underlying cognitive deficit which is the same deficit Frith ascribes to autism. What seems paradoxical about these children makes sense once the autistic pattern is perceived.

In addition, we cannot agree with Bishop's view that the extension of terminology (to view autism in a wider context) is likely to cause more misunderstanding than clarification. We would argue that the reverse is true. The more labels and disorders you provide the more you are going to argue about which child fits into which slot. 'Autism' as a term is widely used because research has shown that the core deficit inherent in the disorder is much more widely spread. It therefore makes good sense to use the term in this way.

Differences between high level autism and language disorder

Autism – high level (Semantic-Pragmatic difficulties)	Language – only
1 Speech and language acquired by 5 years of age, but was delayed.	1 Language acquisition is delayed and deficits persist.
2 Language acquisition does not follow linguistic rules, but rote learned echolalic patterns.	2 Expressive difficulties exceed difficulties with comprehension.
3 Articulatory difficulties are less common.	3 More likely to show dyspraxic elements, i. e. child has articulation difficulties.
4 Echolalic patterns gradually expand ('chunking') – may display skilled use of learnt language and situational speech (mitigated echolalia).	4 Echolalia if present is more likely to be simple and transient.
5 Good auditory memory likely.	5 More likely to make attempts to gain interest of others (sharing of interests, not just attention seeking).
6 Expression is in advance of comprehension.	6 Behaviour generally immature, *not* abnormal or odd.
7 Conversational impairment apparent, i.e. child is unable to maintain interactive communication.	7 More likely to show an even profile apart from language.
8 Likely to talk about own interests. Topics may be odd, range of topics limited.	8 Word finding and word order difficulties apparent – auditory memory skills are poor.
9 Talks at people rather than with people, i. e. does not appear aware of listener's state of mind.	9 Conversational difficulties due to the word finding and word order problems; not an inability to use language appropriately because of an underlying social impairment.
10 Often diagnosed as 'language difficulties and behaviour problems'. Child may be considered	10 Social difficulties due to immaturity *not* underlying deviance.

maladjusted. Underlying social impairment* is *not* recognised – once it is seen, child makes better sense.

11 May or may not be evidence of more overt autism in history. NB Autistic features recede as child develops.

12 Learns easily, but does not necessarily understand and use what is learnt.

13 An uneven profile of skills and deficits. NB Islets of ability.

14 May be hyperlexic *but* there may be dyslexia linked to physical clumsiness (latter associated with Asperger's Syndrome).

15 Play invariably limited, but may impress initially.

16 Uses communication primarily for needs, own interests, etc.

17 Physical milestones likely to be normal and gross motor skills may be good.

11 Likely to show reading difficulties *not* hyperlexia.

12 Play may lack imagination and be immature.

13 Milestones may be delayed – may be gross motor difficulties.

* The term social impairment is used to describe the inability to understand and respond appropriately to the subtleties inherent in varying social situations. It does *not* necessarily mean extreme social isolation or a complete lack of sociability.

At the time of writing, yet another label has emerged, 'High Level Language Disorder' ('HLLD') which not only mirrors the so-called 'Semantic–Pragmatic Disorder', but faithfully describes the communication difficulties of more able autistic children. Many autistic children remain mute. They are likely to be lower functioning. It is generally considered that unless autistic children have acquired some useful speech by the age of five years, the prognosis is less favourable.

WILL SPEECH AND LANGUAGE THERAPY HELP?

Many parents believe that if their autistic child could only be taught to speak, then all would be well. Sadly this is far from reality, and it is essential for speech and language therapists not to inadvertently encourage these expectations in their desire to help.

There is no doubt that speech and language therapists have an important role to play in the diagnosis and assessment of young autistic children. Early recognition of the autistic nature of a young child's communication problems may be crucial in channelling the family towards appropriate agencies that are likely to offer the greatest help. Commonly, autistic children's learnt language and situational speech provide an exaggerated picture of their capabilities in communication. An important aspect of the role of the speech and language therapist is to put these abilities in perspective against the child's level of understanding which may be seriously deficient.

It is our view that it is not necessary to carry out a barrage of formal assessments when the administration of two or three will provide estimations of the child's level of understanding, against which any progress can be monitored. We have found the most useful assessment to be Reynell Developmental Language Scales, The Derbyshire Language Scheme (Detailed Test of Comprehension) as well as The Test of Reception of Grammar, and Renfrew's Action Picture Test and Bus Story.

Linguistic analysis of an autistic child's utterances without heeding the level of comprehension seems to us to be an academic exercise which is largely irrelevant to the practical problems. The idiosyncratic nature of autistic children's use of language is more reliant on auditory memory than true linguistic competence. Therefore we can see little value in minutely examining the output, without first considering the underlying diagnosis and assessing the level of understanding. It is apparent that 'conversations' of higher functioning autistic children may, on first hearing, appear quite impressive. However, those who know the children well will be very aware of the repetitive nature of the exchanges, which reflect particular interests or indeed obsessions. The topics of recorded excerpts of language may be inappropriate or even bizarre, and there is a non-productive quality about the discourse, despite the fact that the child seems capable of changing word order and tenses etc., and using varying and apparently meaningful intonation to produce, at least superficially, the elements of a conversation. The following dialogue illustrates this point:

Background: V, an autistic Asian boy, whose family is conscious of degrees of colour, and their own paleness of skin, is talking to C, a good-looking and very black autistic boy of African origin. It is apparent that J, who is Scottish, and a popular classmate, has provided the trigger for this conversation.

V. C, whereabouts in Scotland do your cousins come from?
C. (Who had recently returned from a holiday) Gatwick!
V. C, are you a little bit white?
C. (Looking carefully at the back of his very black hand) Yes I am a little bit white, because I come from Scotland.
V. Can you speak Scottish?
C. Yes. Hoots!

The provision and necessity for on-going and long-term speech and language therapy is perhaps debatable. The availability of treatment for autistic children from an underfunded and over-stretched profession is likely to vary according to geographical location, financial resources and type of placement. The first two factors are self-explanatory. The third one refers to whether the child is being seen in a community or hospital clinic, has been placed in a playgroup/nursery, or has already entered the education system. In the setting of a clinic, the presumption must be that the child is being investigated and assessed. Any regular treatment is likely to concentrate on advice to the parents about management issues, and the encouragement of communication at the appropriate developmental stage.

Early placement in a nursery or playgroup setting is always to be recommended. This not only provides the child with valuable social experience and learning opportunities, but enables the child's difficulties to be clarified. The speech and language therapist's role in these circumstances may be one of liaison and regular reviews of the child's progress. This naturally leads on to the consideration of a suitable educational placement, which is largely the responsibility of the local education authority, but one in which the speech and language therapist will make a contribution. If it is established that the child has special educational needs, the speech and language therapist will be required to contribute to a formal statement of those needs. This will be discussed in more detail in Chapter 8, on education.

If the child is able to attend a mainstream school, it is less likely that he/she will require speech and language therapy. Within a special school setting, the speech and language therapist is likely to be an adjunct to the class teacher and the role will vary according to the type of school and expertise of the staff. Generally, problems relating to diagnosis will have been resolved, assessment will continue as an on-going process and speech and language therapy treatment will be variable. It is as well to mention at this juncture that the use of the term 'speech therapy' can be very misleading. It suggests that the child is helped to articulate, or talk. As speech therapy offers considerably more than this, a change was made in April 1991 to 'speech and language therapy', which is more suitable and reflects the emphasis on *communication* rather than its elements. Treatment may involve individual or group work, possibly implementing a language programme. Although we are by no means convinced that autistic children necessarily have a fundamental language impairment, there can be little doubt that their lack of motivation to communicate acts as a barrier to the acquisition of language. Therefore the delay can, to some extent, be remediated, in that the child can be moved along to the next developmental stage. For example, a child with a large naming vocabulary may benefit from specific help with the acquisition of verbs. Once again it has to be emphasised that the more able children are most likely to benefit from speech and language therapy input.

More often than not, the most useful approach will be through activities where the emphasis is on extending the child's awareness and understanding of the world about him. Bridges need to be built to enable the child to make at least some links between things that he has learnt. It is of course impossible to provide the child with all the necessary connections. Indeed, if that was the case, he would not be autistic! But at least having some links is better than having none.

Social skills training is another area in which speech and language therapists may be involved. Young children can be taught to improve eye contact, share and take turns, etc., while older children can learn how to go shopping independently, use public transport and develop strategies for behaving appropriately in social situations.

With mute autistic children, attempts have been made to promote communication through the use of manual signs. The most commonly used system is Makaton, which is based on British Sign Language. At one time it was naively believed by some that if these children were taught to sign, they would be able to send out meaningful messages, bypassing their lack of speech. It is now better understood that the underpinnings of language which we have described, as well as a desire to communicate, are necessary requirements for successful signed communication, as indeed they are for spoken language. However, if a mute autistic child learns to produce single signs to indicate his needs, then the teaching of them may be considered worthwhile.

Research has indicated that autistic children do not develop language in the usual way following normal developmental patterns. They appear to acquire language through rote learnt echolalic patterns, and indeed echolalia is a characteristic element in the speech of autistic children. The first speech used by the child may be meaningless echoing of words and phrases. It is necessary to ascertain the degree and complexity of the echolalia and to establish whether it has progressed from the meaningless stage, to one where the stored phrases are used at all appropriately. At the former level, it is not uncommon for the echoing to take the form of hummed tunes, television jingles, or learnt phrases, that either seem pleasing to the ear or appear to carry some emotional content. Even after a child has progressed beyond an echoing stage, he may revert to it in moments of stress and anxiety. In addition, the spontaneously produced speech of many of the more able autistic children seems to consist almost entirely of learnt phrases, often used appropriately, but still giving the speech a mechanical quality. The dividing line between echoing and truly spontaneous speech is often very difficult to define. More able autistic children may break down the echolalia into chunks of varying sizes, and these may then be manipulated so that they result in new utterances.

This has been called 'mitigated echolalia' (Roberts 1989). The children's speech is therefore derivative and the learnt chunks are associated with particular situations, contexts and interests. The child is able to slot them in when need arises and it is evident that if an appropriate verbal trigger is applied, the correct verbal output is elicited. Before children become adept in the use of this strategy, they will give apparently inappropriate responses, because they have made an incorrect choice from their lexicon of learnt language. If the child is capable of using the echolalia/learnt language appropriately, to make a simple dialogue feasible, then this development must be regarded as a communicative success in the context of autism. Indeed, the parameters of successful communication always need to be judged in relation to the child's autism, rather than the expectations of language development in a normal child.

In Chapter 2, we referred to the work of Uta Frith and her colleagues at the Medical Research Council Cognitive Development Unit. Frith has postulated that the fundamental cognitive deficit in autistic children prevents them from predicting the behaviour of other people, a requirement of social competence, which of course includes social communication. This deficit is most clearly seen in more able autistic children with adequate intelligence and adequate understanding of language. Generally, by the age of 4 years, normal children are able to reflect upon their own thoughts and are also becoming aware that other people have thoughts too. In a simple experiment which she and her colleagues developed, the hypothesis was tested with able autistic children, young normal children, and children with Down's Syndrome. The normal children had no difficulty with the test. Even 80 per cent of the Down's Syndrome children passed it, whereas 80 per cent of the autistic children, despite having a higher mental age than the Down's group, failed the test. However, there is evidence that autistic children may pass this test at a later age, but are still likely to fail in more complex tests of perspective taking. These are described by Uta Frith in her book, which was referred to earlier.

For our use and interest we have adapted the basic experiment. We introduce a doll with a basket and a teddy with a box. The doll puts a sweet into her basket and then goes out for a walk. While the doll is out of the way, the teddy takes the sweet and puts it into his box. The doll is then brought back, and wants to eat her sweet. At this point the child, who has been watching all the proceedings, is asked where the doll will look for her sweet. The answer should of course be, in the basket, where the doll put it. Yet autistic children almost invariably point to where *they* know the sweet is, that is, in the box. When they are questioned, they have no difficulty in recalling the sequence of events, but fail to predict what the doll believes. The inability to attribute certain thoughts and beliefs, let alone emotions, to other people will have extreme repercussions, not only in terms of the child's understanding of events and knowledge concerning the world, but in relation to communication. Autistic children's expressive language will reflect this impairment. Simon Baron-Cohen observed that such terms as 'I don't believe you', 'what do you mean?', 'it's not really a...', 'you're just pretending', 'that's not true', 'how do you know?', were likely to be absent.

In linguistic terms, these difficulties occur in the wider context of modality, which relates to possibility, necessity and obligation. Autistic individuals have problems in adapting their learnt and inflexible language to respond to subtle changes in meaning, reflected by the use of modal aspects of language. For example, in relation to auxiliary verbs, the distinctions between can, could, may, might, must, ought to, etc. will present difficulties.

There is overall, even in able autistic people, a quality of naivety and innocence. They are the antithesis of the worldly! They do not deceive others, nor try to impress. Indeed their honesty can be counter-productive. An endearing example of this, is the boy who, when asked by his teacher why he was behaving so badly, replied, 'I was doing it on purpose.'

Frith's explanation of the nature of autism makes sense of the pattern of pragmatic difficulties which are so typical of the language deficits of autistic children, and indeed provides the key to understanding their conversational disabilities.

Chapter 8

Educating autistic children

The implementation of the 1981 Education Act with its emphasis on provision for the individual special needs of each child should assist in the appropriate placement of autistic children according to their overall level and pattern of functioning, rather than focusing solely on the argument of whether they are or are not autistic. In other words, in the context of educational provision, diagnostic labels are not of primary importance. We reiterate our view that by the term 'autistic' we mean a wide spectrum of disabilities and behaviour, encompassing many or few autistic features. We do not limit ourselves to so-called classic cases. Therefore it does not follow that a child diagnosed as autistic will inevitably go to a school for autistic children.

In the last chapter we referred to the process of 'statementing' children with special educational needs. This means that children with identifiable problems that may affect their ability to benefit from mainstream education will have their needs considered by their parents and any professionals who may be involved. It is a pity that this procedure is sometimes presented in a negative way to parents, because the intention is to enable them to express their views and to have as big a say as the professionals in planning their child's future. Apocryphal tales are told of how, in pre-statementing days, children were whisked into special education without sufficient consultation with parents. The statementing system provides a forum for discussion and exchange of views. Indeed, this extract from the Department of Education and Science guidelines for parental involvement states,

> In looking at the child as a whole person, the involvement of the child's parent(s) is essential. Assessment should be seen as a partnership between parents, teachers and other professionals

in a joint endeavour to discover and understand the nature of the difficulties and needs of individual children. Close relations should be established and maintained with parents and can only be helped by frankness and openness on all sides.

This partnership approach is more likely to result in the successful placement of children in schools which cater for their particular needs, regardless of diagnostic labels. Sometimes these special needs can be met within a mainstream school. For example, a physically handicapped child might cope, provided ramps and space are available for a wheelchair. Brighter autistic children may manage in a mainstream school with extra help from a classroom assistant and some remedial teaching; at least for a while. A pragmatic approach to school placement is sensible and, indeed, may be absolutely essential in rural areas, where a low population does not merit a range of different educational options for autistic children. The nearest ideal placement may be at the other end of a county, which would involve two long journeys each day, or a boarding placement which might not be acceptable to parents. Therefore the only practical alternative is to consider whether a more local school can be tailored to meet an individual child's needs. Parents should always be prepared to consider the schools which are available, and ascertain for themselves the setting which will be most suitable for their own child.

It is worthwhile to explore some of the intricacies of the identification, referral, assessment and statementing of children with special educational needs, as those with autism will certainly fall within this category. Many different agencies, including parents as well as doctors, health visitors, speech and language therapists, etc., may identify pre-school children who they believe to be at risk of having educational difficulties. These children may be referred merely for 'informal' assessment, so that the nature of their difficulties will be better understood and their progress monitored. This is only done with parents' consent. Formal referrals, however, are made under the terms of the Education Act 1981, although the children may be referred by the same agencies. The District Health Authority has a responsibility to alert the Education Authority to any child of 2 years or older whom it feels may have special educational needs. If the child is under 2 years, parental consent is required for this to happen. If the child is of school age, formal referral is generally made by the school. A formal assessment usually follows. Information is gathered from various professionals who have been required to assess the child from their own professional perspective. These will include educational psychologists, teachers, speech and language therapists and doctors. The time this process takes is very variable, both between different authorities and even within the same authority. In general the whole process should be completed within six months. If the assessment establishes that the child does have special needs, the authority is required by law to meet these needs either by making additional resources available to a mainstream school, or by providing education in a special school or unit. Such decisions are made by the Special Educational Needs Panel within each Education Authority.

Ideally the Education Authority will keep parents fully informed about the proceedings and will certainly invite them to express their own views about their child's particular needs at this time. Parents may also submit any other information which they feel has a bearing on their child's needs. They are given twenty-nine days to make their submission before the formal assessment begins. Inevitably some authorities are reluctant to accommodate particular needs or make sufficient resources available. It is possible under such circumstances for parents to appeal. The Advisory Centre for Education will be able to provide information about the procedure. Under the best of circumstances the statement should precede a child's entry into special education. If both parents and the Special Educational Needs Panel are in agreement, a child can have an 'assessment placement' in the recommended setting before the statementing procedure has been completed.

We have already explained that autistic children do not necessarily attend schools specifically for autistic children. We know now how variable autistic children may be, both in their academic capabilities as well as in their behaviour. The autistic children who are likely to be able to cope in mainstream education will be those who are more mildly affected. Typically, they do not show behaviour abnormalities which would make them conspicuous. They will have acquired language which they are generally able to use appropriately. In addition, their academic capabilities will be within normal limits. Sometimes such children survive in mainstream because of the provision of a classroom assistant who ensures that the autistic child is enabled to function despite his problems. The assistant may ease the child's path in ways such as ensuring that he does what he is supposed to do, understands instructions properly, and is not teased or bullied in the playground. Some children will only manage in mainstream for a period of their school lives, and much depends on the attitudes of the headteacher and staff. It must be acknowledged that as the child moves up in the school, more will be expected of him. Some autistic children manage well at the infant level, but when the move is made to junior school begin to flounder, as there are different expectations and more demands are made of them in terms of independence and organisation, both socially and in relation to school work. We do not believe that a mildly autistic child should continue in mainstream at all costs. The paramount concern must surely be the child's happiness and quality of life. If, despite adequate academic capability, a child's life is dominated by stress and anxiety, then serious consideration should be given to an alternative placement. Although the academic expectations may be less, the child's overall happiness and well-being may be considerably enhanced. We believe that this is equally, if not more, important.

It is not unknown for an Education Authority to finance an intellectually able autistic child's attendance at a small independent mainstream school, which may provide a more structured and less confusing educational setting. It is imperative that parents do not allow a situation to develop whereby withdrawal from mainstream education is viewed as a failure by either them, or their child. Mildly autistic children may be very aware of success and failure and it is therefore incumbent upon the parents to explain any move in positive terms.

The number of overtly autistic children who may be considered likely candidates for mainstream education is very small indeed. The majority of the autistic population will have a greater or lesser degree of mental handicap. Sadly, most are severely mentally handicapped. Although autism has been found to occur in children of all levels of intelligence, there is ample evidence to show that this is the most important prognostic factor in an autistic child. Although teaching and therapy may improve the level of functioning, it will make little difference to the IQ score. Therefore, special education is more likely to be required for the vast majority of children with a clear diagnosis of autism.

A substantial number of more mildly affected autistic children have difficulties which from the outset may preclude them from mainstream education. This group does not show much, if any, overtly bizarre behaviour. They are viewed as odd, quirky or eccentric, and the autistic nature of their difficulties has often not been recognised. Their problems appear to centre around their use of language, which may have been delayed, as well as their poor social skills. Although we would argue that these children do not generally suffer from a language disorder *per se*, they certainly have communication problems. They may have acquired adequate language, but do not know how to use it. They often fit very well into schools for language disordered children or into Local Education Authority language units. These settings provide small group teaching and structure and the proximity of socially normal peers enables the autistic children to learn at least some acceptable social behaviour from more appropriate role models. Such placements will be successful if the staff appreciate that, although the needs of this group of children differ in some ways from those of the specifically speech and language disordered group, they can be managed successfully together.

We would recommend a category of 'communication disorder/difficulty' as an appropriate designation for schools to cater for children with speech and language problems as well as children with a milder degree of autism. This would eliminate arguments about labels and would provide a background for on-going diagnostic assessment. First-hand experience of such a school over a number of years, has provided ample evidence of the good sense of such a classification.

Sometimes, schools for children with moderate learning difficulties (MLD) are suitable for autistic children who do not present with behaviour that is difficult to manage. Again, successful placement depends very much on the ethos of the school and the interest and attitudes of the staff. When a school is well disposed to the needs of an autistic child, favourable progress is much more likely.

The majority of children diagnosed as autistic are severely mentally handicapped and consequently will have severe learning difficulties. There is no reason why such children should not be placed in schools which cater for this group and, indeed, many schools known to us are doing this very successfully. As low functioning autistic children often display particularly difficult behaviour, education authorities have to appreciate that extra resources may be required to facilitate the successful management of such children. Sometimes parents of severely autistic children are very distressed that their child should be considered in the context of mental handicap, especially if that child displays any islets of ability. It has to be acknowledged that the child's level of intellectual functioning must inevitably be regarded as the prime consideration. The presence of autism is an added dimension, that complicates the picture and may lead to conflicting appraisals of the child's capabilities and potential. It is not unknown for schools to underestimate their suitability for dealing with autistic children. They assume that they should be providing something extra special. In our experience, the provision of 'outreach' support (this is utilising the skills and experience of specialist professionals in an advisory capacity outside their own centres) enables them to feel more confident in understanding, managing and educating autistic children.

We must not forget the important role The National Autistic Society has played in the establishment of education for autistic children. They continue to provide a number of schools, both day and boarding, as well as some provision for young adults. In general, Society schools provide placements for children with moderate or severe learning difficulties, who in addition, present behaviour problems that make placement in less specialised settings unlikely.

All statemented children are reviewed annually. This means that their progress is evaluated, and the suitability of their school placement is considered again. It is possible that the child's needs will have changed and that different and more appropriate provision may be necessary. This review procedure has the advantage of reminding everybody concerned that even though a child has been placed in a particular educational setting, the situation may change, and should not be regarded as static.

The present philosophy and methods of teaching autistic children have developed over the years and reflect better understanding of the nature of the disorder. During the 1960s and early 1970s, it was assumed that autistic children were invariably of normal intelligence, their difficulties arising from an inability to communicate because of some sort of emotional 'block'. Many schools were established in the belief that intensive education intervention would 'break through the barrier' of non-communication and allow these children to develop normally. It became apparent that these optimistic expectations were ill-founded and nowadays a more realistic attitude prevails.

Autistic children commonly show pseudo-academic skills such

as mechanical reading or calculation abilities. It was natural for educationalists to assume that these represented the child's true potential. We now know that, remarkable though these skills may be, the child remains severely handicapped and is not able to utilise these abilities in the normal way. The pursuit of academic goals is no longer seen as the only priority and the development of life skills has assumed greater importance in the curriculum. These will include independence training and self-care, shopping and cooking simple meals, as well as other everyday activities which the normal population take so much for granted.

The introduction of the National Curriculum will challenge the teachers of autistic children to provide as wide an educational experience as possible, while acknowledging the particular difficulties of the children they are teaching. The Association of Head Teachers of Autistic Children and Adults have to date produced two booklets entitled *The Special Curricular Needs of Autistic Children*. These can be obtained from the Association (the address is listed in Appendix 2, pp. 119–21). In addition, the National Autistic Society has published papers directed at teachers, about access to the National Curriculum for autistic children.

Sometimes autistic children make good academic progress and a structured and formal learning situation is much to their liking. Many have little difficulty with the mechanics of reading and may score extremely well on word recognition tests above their chronological age and well in excess of their other abilities. Yet, when it comes to understanding what they have so ably read, they display severe deficits. This is particularly evident when meaning is embedded and information is implied rather than explicit. The term 'hyperlexia' has been used to describe this prodigious ability. An example of this phenomenon was a little boy of 6 years who received a party invitation which he read perfectly, yet had no idea what it was or what it meant. Parents are sometimes perturbed because a teacher appears to be holding back their child's reading. However, unless the written material is meaningful to the child, the reading of it will become one more skill that will have no real value. Therefore, the child's comprehension should always be matched to his mechanical reading ability.

Depending on their level of functioning, autistic children may have no difficulty with the mechanics of writing. Although more able children can be taught to produce properly constructed sentences, they will be unable to use the skill with true creative ability.

However, at the upper end of the autistic continuum, there are children who appear to demonstrate aspects of creativity in their writing, but the topics remain eccentric, bizarre or repetitive. Again, depending on intellectual ability, autistic children may develop number concepts and be able to calculate. It has been observed that numeracy skills may exist as yet another islet of ability.

Dr Lorna Selfe has made a study of art and autism and has observed that there are a small number of autistic children who display an amazing ability with line drawing, and whose development of drawing skills has been 'totally anomalous'. She concludes that what these children may be doing is 'translating visual experience into drawing, untrammelled by normal conceptual analysis and reorganisation.' It is as if the child records as a camera. Stephen Wiltshire's book of remarkable pen drawings of city buildings, with minute attention to detail, bears this out.

It is by no means unknown for parents of children who do not progress well to blame their child's teacher. Although parental disappointment is very understandable, it has to be accepted that those autistic children who make most progress do so by virtue of inherent developmental factors rather than any special teaching or treatment methods. Despite this somewhat gloomy comment, we have witnessed great progress in individual children and can applaud the innovative and persistent approaches which many teachers demonstrate in their daily contact with autistic children.

ACTIVITIES OUTSIDE SCHOOL

Activities outside school and home are a normal part of the majority of children's lives, and there is no reason why autistic children should not participate in them as well. Because the condition is so variable it is not possible to be specific about activities which will be successful for all children on the autistic continuum. Apart from individual likes and dislikes, the degree of mental handicap as well as possible behaviour difficulties must be taken into account when choices are made. However, most certainly, something will be available if parents are prepared to search about in their own locality. The societies set up for the mentally handicapped may have much to offer which will be appropriate for autistic children and young people. Other facilities may be provided by associations for more specific impairments such as dyslexia: these too may be suitable for other groups of children with difficulties.

Many higher functioning autistic children, although unable to cope in mainstream education, may benefit greatly from opportunities to mix with their normal peers. Out of school activities will help them to develop an awareness of the larger world outside. They will learn to share, take turns, etc., in a setting where fewer allowances are made for them. Organisations such as Cubs, Brownies and Woodcraft Folk are often very willing to include an autistic child in their packs and are very responsive to the special needs of individual children. It is important for parents to be open and honest, and prepared to take group leaders into their confidence in order to maximise the chances of success both for their child and for the group itself.

Other activities which, in our experience, have been successful for particular children are trampolining, gymnastics, swimming and dancing as well as horse riding. Drama and art classes are less likely to be suitable, as creativity and imagination are areas of difficulty for autistic individuals. Parents need to be very flexible in finding the activity which is right for their child. For example, a child who loved to dance failed as a ballet dancer because she was unable to count steps. In the informality of disco dancing, however, she blossomed.

Older children who show a liking for social contact may enjoy attending youth clubs, providing that they are well run and adequately supervised. Again, in this area, many of the parent support organisations provide facilities which may be tapped. Activity holidays for older children with handicaps are available and are worth investigating. There is no reason why autistic children should not enjoy the achievements of abseiling, as well as canoeing, camping, climbing and other outdoor pursuits.

Chapter 9

Growing up – what lies beyond?

Almost as soon as parents learn that their child may be autistic, their thoughts inevitably turn to the future – what will the outcome be? Because of the 'loss' of the normal child, there is a need to reconstruct a future which takes account of the changed circumstances, and this is very understandable. Parents will couch their enquiries with phrases such as 'I know it's asking too much, but what will happen when he/she is grown up?' or 'Will he get better?', 'Will he be able to get a job and be independent?', 'Will he get married and have children?' and 'Are we always going to have to look after him?'

While autism in adolescents and adults is beyond our brief, we feel that we cannot ignore what is clearly a fundamental issue arising out of the diagnosis.

At the outset, it is perhaps worth pointing out that looking into the future of normal children is also fraught with imponderables, as many parents know. The bright, articulate 5-year-old who subsequently does brilliantly in school, in adolescence may become wayward and rebellious and the academic future with high expectations dissipates. The potential brain surgeon becomes a lorry driver, while the slow starter emerges as a skilled entrepreneur. Parents of all children suffer disappointments, worry and frustration when the expectations for their children fail to materialise. Concern about drugs, sexual promiscuity and orientation, smoking, dropping-out, etc. are additional anxieties which parents of normal teenage children have to contend with. Although the time of growing up is worrying for the parents of normal children, for parents with handicapped children the concerns are greatly increased and additionally there is an extra dimension of concern, which is 'What will happen when we are gone, or too old to look after him?'. The normal expectation for parents is that their children will grow up and leave home sooner or later, allowing parents some time in middle age to enjoy the freedom and opportunities which life has to offer. For the parents of handicapped children, this scenario is at odds with the likely prolongation of the parental caring role into their child's adulthood. It is for this reason that we recommend that parents are in touch with organisations which can offer help and advice, while addressing these issues.

The National Autistic Society has published a list of establishments specifically for autistic adolescents and adults. Some are run by the National Autistic Society, and some by local autistic societies. In addition the Society provides a comprehensive list of organisations which run centres for people with learning difficulties which have occasionally accepted residents with autism. Many of these are registered charities.

Local Authority funding may be obtained for placements in communities run by voluntary organisations or independent companies. However, the National Autistic Society does not monitor these establishments and therefore cannot recommend any particular organisations to families.

The decisions parents make about the future for their older autistic child will reflect their own personal circumstances and philosophy as well as availability of facilities and resources. What is right or acceptable for one couple may be quite unacceptable and totally at odds with the views of another. Compromise may be possible for some, but not for others. Some parents feel very strongly that they want to keep their child at home with them for as long as possible. Others welcome the chance for their child to leave home and lead a separate life as soon as the opportunity arises. There is no right or wrong about this, nor should there be any feelings of guilt or failure if parents do decide not to keep their grown-up child at home. We recommend that parents keep an open mind and start to consider the options earlier rather than later. Often there are waiting lists, and putting the child's name forward may increase his chances of being considered for placement when the time comes. We feel that it is not too early to start thinking ahead constructively when the child is about 13–14 years of age. Visits to different establishments, when there is no pressure to make decisions, are often the best way to evaluate the kind of setting where an individual autistic young person is likely to be happy and enjoy a lifestyle which parents feel is appropriate for his needs. This is particularly so in relation to young people going to live in a community.

We must again remind readers that autistic children are very variable, and therefore the outcome will also be variable. At the lower end of the autistic continuum, which will include individuals who are not only autistic but who have a severe mental handicap, the picture will be much the same as for the mentally handicapped non-autistic population. Such people are likely to require care and support throughout their lives. This may be in a variety of settings, either day or residential. Some of these may be specifically for autistic individuals and are geared towards coping with the behaviour problems associated with autism. Those young people who can cope, may find places in Local Authority residential homes, where they function as a group with supervision and support. This means that they can live apart from their families, enjoy social activities and have a purposeful routine of daily attendance at an Adult Training Centre or sheltered workshop.

More able autistic young people may well be able to attend post-school courses at Tertiary or Further Education Colleges. These courses are specially aimed at young people with special needs, and there will be emphasis on the teaching of life skills. The curriculum may include solo shopping expeditions, cooking simple meals, coping with transport, gaining work experience and learning to manage finances at a basic level. There are also residential courses where the content is much the same as we have described. The aim is the promotion of independence, as well as the enhancement of social development. Sadly, despite the excellence of these courses, the student at the end of his time is likely to find himself in limbo. Unless further plans have been made, he may find himself back at home with his family and with the prospects of employment virtually non-existent.

The more we learn about autism, the more we have become aware that within the normal population there are individuals with social difficulties of an autistic nature. These may be serious enough for the individual himself to feel that he has problems, not only in regard to his social life, but also in relation to the work place. It is likely that others will regard such people as being particularly gauche, odd, eccentric and somehow difficult to get on with. If this is the situation for people who are within the normal population, it is hardly surprising that those whose difficulties have been, or are, severe enough to be considered autistic have more testing problems to contend with.

However sympathetic supervisors and fellow workers may be, the most able of the autistic population, despite adequate intelligence and the acquisition of many useful skills, with certain exceptions, fail to survive in the world of employment.

The National Autistic Society/Department of Health and Social Security published a report in 1984 entitled 'The Natural History of Able Autistic People'. It recorded that sadly this group, despite earlier optimism, tended to need the support and structure provided by Adult Training Centres, which is in fact where the majority were best placed.

Why is it that, despite so much costly input and despite the acquisition of so many skills, the overtly autistic young person more often than not fails to adapt or cope in the real world? It has to be recognised that the special area of difficulty in autism – the social impairment – is an incapacity which is fundamentally detrimental to securing and holding down a job. For example, pre-occupations with routines may make it difficult to work alongside other people. The lack of ability to adapt to changes – to hurry, to complete a task, to see things from another's point of view – although seemingly trivial factors, can combine to form real obstacles to success. Unfortunately, there is a dearth of suitable placements for autistic young people which will harness their skills while coping with and managing their difficulties.

Sometimes the best possible placements are in community settings. These may be Village Communities in a rural location, but may also be in residential urban areas where accommodation and support is provided in a house adapted for this purpose. Within such communities the autistic individual may flourish and parents can feel that, as the young person establishes a home there, the burden of responsibility is lifted.

Chapter 10

A postscript – alternative treatments and cures for autism?

At the outset, we have to express extreme scepticism about the effectiveness of any of the alternative treatments/therapies/cures that we have come upon. We cannot see that there can possibly be a panacea for such a variable condition with so many different causes. It is, of course, reasonable to suppose that certain approaches may benefit particular children. However, to expect that such a complex and multifaceted condition as autism can be cured by a single method or drug really makes little sense.

It is understandable that when parents hear that their young child is autistic, they are so anxious to help him/her, that they are very vulnerable indeed to those expressing unrestrained claims for a cure. We do deplore those who take advantage of this situation by promoting their views with immoderate zeal. We do not doubt that enthusiasts for these treatments are well meaning, but in our view the promotion of a cure without back-up of facts and figures (rather than anecdotes) is not good enough. Neither is their insistence that the 'autistic establishment' is biased against them a good enough response to criticism. Unless claims for successful treatment can be supported by objective evidence, parents and professionals should continue to remain sceptical and wary. It is often reported that the introduction of a new regime, be it school, drug or diet, can bring about significant improvements, but unfortunately such spurts are not maintained.

We have already referred to the administration of certain vitamins and drugs in Chapter 3, in which we discussed the causes of autism. None of these medication programmes have proved to be successful, despite some early optimism. Additionally, allergies to certain foods have provided another possible explanation for the presence of autism. Avoidance of particular foods such as chocolate, milk and milk products, as well as such additives as tartrazine, has brought about an improvement in the behaviour of some children, but not cured the condition. Tartrazine has been linked to hyperactivity in children, and so it would seem wise for parents to eliminate this substance from their children's diet. The subject of additives and allergies is quite rightly an area for concern to the population in general, and it is worthwhile for parents of autistic children to note whether episodes of particular behaviour can be linked to certain foods or possible environmental factors.

In the same chapter we also mentioned holding therapy, which has received much publicity in the media. What possibly lies behind claims for improvement in some children is the fact that during holding therapy there is considerable physical activity while the child struggles and rages. This coincides with observations that, after vigorous physical exercise, autistic children tended to have periods of good behaviour. It is possible therefore that Bernard Rimland's suggestion that 'holding does not restore maternal/infant bonds, but rather stimulates the brain's production of endorphins' is a reasonable explanation. Endorphins are naturally occurring substances which are produced by the brain and have the effect of controlling anxiety.

Another approach with emphasis on vigorous exercise as an integral part of the curriculum is used at Dr Kiyo Kitahara's Higashi School in Boston, USA. The original Higashi School was established in Tokyo in 1954. The ethos of the school is based on 'daily life therapy' which keeps the children occupied and controlled during weekdays, although there is surprisingly little activity during weekends. As well as physical exercise, art and music are important components of the curriculum, while the promotion of language skills is not a central part of it. Imitation of role models is advocated, using both teachers and more advanced pupils. The school promotes a group approach, rather than programmes tailored to the individual. Children with physical problems serious enough to prevent them from participating in physical exercises are excluded from the school.

Until now there has been no independent evaluation of the Higashi School. Many questions need to be asked about the educational curriculum, and about the efficacy of 'daily life therapy' in the long term, especially as extravagant claims have been made by advocates of the school's approach, much promoted by the media. The National Autistic Society will shortly be publishing the findings of its evaluation of the Higashi method, and will be in a position to offer parents information if they are considering the school for their children. Before selling their homes and crossing the Atlantic parents should consider investigating the schools in this country. They may be much encouraged by what they find.

More recently, the 'Option Approach' has emerged, again in the United States. The philosophy of this approach is that feelings are governed by attitudes. If attitudes can be changed, then feelings will change. 'We can choose to be happy', i.e. happy with an autistic child. Parents are offered considerable support and encouragement in an emotionally loving and caring setting, when they are introduced to the method. In our view, this is very positive and acceptable. However, the practice of this philosophy involves such extreme changes in family life that for us the credibility of the approach is lost. Briefly, the child is enclosed in a separate room in the family home, where he controls everything that happens to him. He is attended by a team of volunteers, working on the basis of child initiated activities, throughout his waking hours.

Any teacher or therapist working with autistic children over a number of years will be able to claim many successes. However, we know of no one who is prepared to assert that they have cured the condition. Within the natural history of the disorder, children will make progress, sometimes with and sometimes without intervention. The provision therefore in many schools attended by autistic children may achieve comparable results without any accompanying publicity and propaganda. It has been established that autistic children make greater progress in schools where there is structure and routine rather than in settings where creativity, free expression and imagination are given greater priority.

Aversion therapy should perhaps be mentioned in the context of children displaying very severe behaviour problems such as self-injury and aggression. It has been more commonly practised in the United States, rather than this country. It involves the use of an unpleasant stimulus to reduce undesirable behaviour. The application of such methods would be abhorrent to most people, and their use could be deemed unethical. In addition, there is little evidence of improvement over the long term if the therapy is suspended. Positive techniques for managing extreme behaviour have been successful, but the debate continues.

It is not uncommon for the difficulties of higher functioning autistic children to go unrecognised and instead be seen in terms of emotional disturbance and/or poor parental management. For this reason, some of these children and their families are referred for family therapy, or else the child is seen by a psychotherapist and treatment may be prescribed. Sometimes the treatment programmes are offered because the autism is not recognised. But in some cases psychotherapy is offered on the basis that autism has an underlying emotional cause. As far as family therapy is concerned, it seems to us that failure to recognise the nature of the child's difficulties does little to inspire confidence in this approach amongst those with experience of the condition. Nor do we think it is helpful to give parents the idea that their child's problems are caused by their mismanagement, rather than an organic condition. It must be said, though, that when the condition is recognised, the entire family can benefit from discussion about how best to manage the autistic individual and this approach may then be helpful and constructive.

Over the years, we have come across a small number of autistic children receiving psychotherapy. In some of these cases, the autism was not acknowledged and the children's difficulties were considered to be emotional in origin despite, in addition, accompanying mental handicap, even to a severe degree. In other cases the autism was acknowledged, yet thought to be treatable by this method. One could argue endlessly and inconclusively about whether the child's educational and managment regime in school had brought about improvement, or whether the claims of the psychotherapist had any substance. We can only make comments based on our own experience of individual cases. These suggest that psychotherapy is not an appropriate treatment for autism, and the claims made for its efficacy reflect optimism in the mind of the therapist, rather than actual evidence in the child. It is all too easy to project thoughts and feelings on to a child with seriously limited communication, and to make interpretations of anomalous behaviour, based on analytical theory.

There is a small percentage of parents who cannot be helped by traditional methods and who feel compelled to try approaches which are outside what they regard as the autistic establishment. Often it is this 'establishment' which has made the diagnosis of autism. Understandably, these parents' feelings of upset and anger are then directed towards this body. It is as if the messenger bearing the bad news is to be blamed, and therefore any help that is offered is not acceptable.

Within the alternative approaches there may be much which is perfectly sensible and reasonable and indeed may provide some amelioration of some of the facets of autism. Different parents have different needs in the type and amount of support they may require. If they feel happy and comfortable with a certain approach, then it will be of benefit to them, even if it is not of great benefit to the child.

Early in 1991, a dictionary of different approaches to the treatment of autism was published by the National Autistic Society Autism Research Unit. It aims to provide a description of all the known approaches together with contact addresses. Evaluations are included where they have been carried out and regular updates are envisaged. It is worth mentioning that the Nottingham University Child Development Research Unit is also evaluating alternative approaches for autism, and their data should be completed in 1992.

It is most regrettable that a considerable number of professionals involved with young children do not recognise autism, and even if it is recognised there is an absence of support in many parts of the country. It is very likely that alternative methods of treatment fill this gap and indicate the grievous deficits which often exist in locally provided educational and medical services. Many parents, even in an area of relatively good awareness and support, have said, 'Okay, we know our 2-year-old is autistic, but what now?'. Ideally, we would like to see the provision of specialist nurseries, where young children with autistic features could attend, even on a part-time basis, for on-going assessment. In this way, expertise in autism would be centralised within a district, and parents would have access to advice and support. Until this sort of provision is more widely available, we do urge all parents to adopt a questioning stance before embarking on any so-called cure or treatment which is not based on a realistic assessment of the child's overall functioning.

Appendix 1

CASE STUDIES

The following case histories, although based on real children, have been altered in certain ways to protect identity and ensure anonymity. The cases described reflect the wide-range of presentation within the autistic continuum.

Tanya: now aged 6+ years

Referral

Tanya's initial referral was to the community speech and language therapist for non-development of language. Autistic features were noted and there was a subsequent referral to the specialist speech and language therapist within the district, who wrote the following report when Tanya was aged 4 years.

Background information

Tanya is the fourth child of parents from Eastern Europe. The older children have no problems and attend mainstream schools. A mixture of English and German is spoken in the home.

Early development and medical history

Tanya was a very difficult baby and it was only later, with hindsight, that it was apparent that subtle developmental abnormalities were present, but remained unrecognised. Tanya's physical development and milestones were normal, in spite of which her mother sensed that all was not well and that somehow Tanya was different.

As she had three other children, Tanya's undiscriminating friend-liness to strangers was ascribed to a personality difference, rather than a symptom of abnormal social development.

From an early age, Tanya showed an interest in electrical ap-pliances. In the past she has used an adult's arm as a tool, but this is no longer apparent.

It was reported that Tanya displayed certain skills which she then lost – such as counting objects, etc.

Tanya will occupy herself for long periods and is able to engage in symbolic play (feeding, washing dolls, etc.) but cannot develop it creatively. There is no history of any serious medical conditions. At one stage, there was a query about Tanya's hearing ability, due to her failure to alert consistently. It has been observed that Tanya will put her hands over her ears on learning loud or unusual noises. She enjoys listening to music.

Appearance

Tanya is a very attractive and dainty little girl with an alert and enquiring expression. She has good eye contact and superficially appears normal. However, careful observation reveals a number of small behavioural abnormalities which include odd hand pos-tures and some body twirling.

Behaviour

Generally Tanya's behaviour could be described as immature. Until very recently she had an obsessive interest in a particular video which she would insist on watching continually. She has also shown a sustained interest in particular books, which she would look at *ad nauseam*. Recently, Tanya has become aware of shadows and at the moment this is a focus of interest for her. It has been observed that Tanya will come up close to people and stare at them. She habitually carries round a baby bottle for drinking and for apparent comfort.

Sociability

Generally, Tanya does not like being touched. At nursery, she will play alongside other children, but not *with* them. Her earlier lack of discrimination towards people has been replaced by clinging to her mother and objecting to being left, although this reaction is now diminishing.

General management and problems

As mentioned earlier, Tanya is a difficult child to manage. She does not go to bed until 10.00 or 11.00 p.m., yet it is very difficult to rouse her in the mornings. For this reason, she attends the nursery in the afternoons. Tanya is toilet trained, and will take down her own knickers if encouraged. She is exceedingly fussy about food and mealtimes are particularly difficult. Her difficult behaviour and parental feelings of guilt, if not shame, about her handicap, have led to the family isolating themselves from contact with friends and neighbours.

Attention control

Tanya is able to concentrate on tasks which interest her for a considerable period of time.

Cognitive development

No formal assessments have been carried out. On visual perceptual tasks, Tanya shows capability. She holds a pencil very well and can colour in. She can name colours and will sometimes use them as labels for objects.

Speech and language

No formal language assessments have been carried out. Generally, Tanya is spoken to in English at home, to avoid confusion. It is likely that Tanya's language comprehension skills are limited. She is able to label objects and apply some learnt and situational phrases to obtain her needs. Some echolalia is evident.

Conclusion

The profile of Tanya's developmental abnormalities and social and communication impairments is consistent with a diagnosis of autism.

Update

Tanya's parents were understandably upset by the diagnosis of autism, and this was complicated by the fact that a parallel referral to a Child Development Centre resulted in a different diagnosis of 'severe communication problem'. Speech and language therapy was prescribed and the idea was promoted that this would solve Tanya's problems. This confused the parents and did not provide a satisfactory explanation for Tanya's diverse difficulties. Meanwhile, referral had been made to an appropriate school for higher functioning autistic children, which was able to offer much support and guidance before Tanya's admission there. A subsequent meeting between the professional agencies involved with the family, resulted in agreement and better understanding about the true nature of Tanya's difficulties. A unified approach was agreed upon, which has proved to be both acceptable and productive.

The family was encouraged to participate in social activities once again, which was important for the other children whose needs were being ignored while the focus of attention was on Tanya. Tanya herself was in need of more social contact to widen her experience, and this has been of great benefit to her as well.

Once Tanya was admitted to the school some four months later, more formal assessments were undertaken. At the age of 4 years 4 months, her understanding of language scored at 2 years 2 months, and her expressive language scored at 2 years 1 month. Six months later, her comprehension had not improved, but some progress had been made with expression and there was an increase in the use of situational speech. It was very difficult to get her to attend to tasks which were not of her choice. Great progress was made at this time with Tanya's eating habits, using a structured programme which was also carried out at home. Subsequently, her physical appearance became more robust. Her behaviour improved and her temper tantrums decreased. Further language assessment at the age of 5 years 9 months resulted in a comprehension score of 3 years 9 months and an expressive score of 3 years 1 month. The most recent assessment at age 6 years 4 months shows a slight acceleration of progress, with scores for both comprehension and expression of 4 years 7 months. Tanya's attention is now entirely satisfactory and she is making good progress with reading and number skills. She now plays *with* other children in her class group, and has started attending integration sessions in a mainstream school, which have so far been successful.

Tanya now presents as a somewhat 'quaint' child. On first encounter she may seem normal. She gives information, asks questions, and the idiosyncracies in her behaviour have diminished. However, it does become apparent that there is a repetitive quality about her activities and communication so that, although great progress has been made, it would be unrealistic to presume that Tanya will ever cease to show autistic features.

We have no reason to doubt that she will continue to make good progress, and it is felt that increasing contact with normal children will provide her with good models on which to pattern her own behaviour.

Hannah: now aged 5 years 9 months

Referral

Hannah was referred to the community speech and language therapist for delayed language development. Autistic features were observed, and Hannah was consequently referred to a specialist speech and language therapist. This report was written when Hannah was 2 years of age.

Background information

Hannah is the daughter of an English mother and a Turkish father. Her older brother had a congenital abnormality, affecting his digestive system, but was otherwise normal. Hannah's birth history and early development are reported to have been entirely uneventful and her developmental milestones were normal. However, careful questioning of Hannah's mother revealed that, in retrospect, some subtle indications of abnormal social development were evident from an early age. She is reported to have been a very 'good' baby who did not appear to initiate social interaction nor show reciprocity. There was an early interest in television and video knobs, yet Hannah's attention could not be gained when picture books were introduced. Hannah's responses were different from those of her elder brother, but at this stage they were explained away by the belief that she simply had a different personality. The parents were not seriously concerned about her development until Hannah was around 18 months old, when her lack of alerting behaviour to speech prompted investigations for the possibility of a hearing loss. It was obvious though that Hannah had no difficulty in responding to sounds that were of interest to her. For example, the television being turned on when she was in another room. Subsequent investigations revealed that her hearing was normal.

It is reported by her mother that Hannah has never established a good sleeping pattern. Recently this has deteriorated and is now the main management problem and is causing concern. Hannah is not yet toilet trained and shows no signs of awareness. More significantly perhaps, her mother has observed that Hannah does not seem able to anticipate the outcome of daily routines, for example, that putting on her coat is a preliminary to going on an outing – an activity which she particularly enjoys.

In response to further questions, some hand flapping was reported, as well as tiptoe walking, and very poor eye contact. Hannah dislikes any intrusion into her own activities, but will indicate to her mother an occasional desire for cuddles. This extends to enjoyment of rough and tumble play. Generally, however, she could be described as aloof and self-contained.

General observations

Hannah is a most attractive little girl of normal appearance, who is physically well developed and seems rather older than her chronological age of barely 2 years. During an observation session, when no formal assessment was attempted, Hannah occupied herself with the toys that were available. However, her play consisted of handling and moving items around, rather than any meaningful activity. It is reported that she enjoys using bricks and can construct, showing considerable dexterity. Her 'play' was accompanied by constant vocalising, which included intonation patterns and babble, but there was no recognisable speech and language. Hannah is indifferent to all attempts at social interaction. No bizarre behaviour has been observed.

Conclusions and indications

Hannah's pattern of developmental abnormality, encompassing social impairment and language delay, suggests autism is an appropriate term to describe her spectrum of difficulties. Although Hannah was seen on a number of occasions at a major teaching hospital, no diagnosis was offered and both parents were anxious to know what was the matter with Hannah. It seemed appropriate, therefore, when Hannah's mother requested a diagnosis, having expressed exasperation with the hospital, to suggest autism. Some information was provided about the nature of the condition, and the parents seemed relieved that at last there was an explanation for their puzzling daughter.

Update

Despite initial euphoria at having a diagnosis, when the parents found out more about the condition they became angry and depressed. They found fault with the way the diagnosis had been given, even though they themselves had requested it. The community speech and language therapist, who saw Hannah regularly, was able to offer some on-going support while arrangements were made for Hannah to see the community paediatrician and educational psychologist for assessment. At this time it was assumed that Hannah's developmental progress was not seriously delayed, and indeed when she was seen again by the specialist speech and language therapist five months later, some progress had been made. Body twirling, however, was much in evidence, but Hannah was beginning to imitate some situational words such as 'bye-bye' and 'again'. Generally, management had become less of a problem and Hannah was beginning to anticipate routine events, such as getting ready for play group. Her mother appeared to have come to terms with the diagnosis, but expressed extreme sadness and it was felt that she would be very vulnerable to unwise counsel and promises of a cure for autism. Although the parents wished to make their home in Turkey, lack of provision of special education there made them decide to stay in the UK for the time being.

In the meantime, the parents attended a support group at the school which, it was presumed, would later provide for Hannah's educational needs. Hannah was reviewed again at the age of 4 years when it was very obvious that, regardless of the autistic features, Hannah had severe learning difficulties. This was yet another blow for the parents, who now had to come to terms with the fact that Hannah was not only autistic but also severely mentally handicapped. This blow revived all their former anger, especially when an alternative educational placement was deemed more suitable for Hannah's needs. The school suggested was for children with severe learning difficulties, a fact which the parents took some time to come to terms with. However, as the school was particularly well run and well equipped, the place was accepted and Hannah has settled well and made progress. She continued to develop some language, although only for her own needs.

When Hannah was 6 years old, the family finally decided to leave the UK and went to settle in Turkey.

Jason: now aged 6 years

Referral

Jason was referred for speech and language therapy by his mother at the age of 3 years 8 months, when she became aware that his language was not developing normally. This report was written two months later.

Background information

Although there was nothing untoward in Jason's developmental history, he appears small for his age, and generally functions as a child younger than his chronological age. Both fine and gross motor control are immature, although he shows good capability in self-help skills. Jason has attended a nursery school since before his third birthday.

Attention control

This is very satisfactory indeed, when Jason is provided with tasks which interest him and are within his capability. When tasks are beyond him, he opts out and refuses to co-operate.

Symbolic understanding

Jason has no difficulty in this area and was able to score fully in the Lowe and Costello Symbolic Play Test, although it must be pointed out that the ceiling score is at a 3 year level. However, Jason appears unable to develop play imaginatively, and when observed, merely repeated a single play 'routine' and displayed no interest in utilising the play materials he was given.

Social development

Jason enjoys the company of other children and responds to them but is not able to initiate or play imaginatively with them. He has been described as 'solitary' and will spend time looking at books rather than involving himself with his peers. There is no doubt that he enjoys nothing better than sitting down with an adult and being directed to perform the sort of tasks in which he shows capability. However, in school, when left to his own devices, he does not seek out constructive means of occupying himself, and will sit and look about until an adult intervenes.

Speech and language

It was reported that when Jason started at the nursery his comprehension of language was very limited indeed and his utterances consisted of single words.

Assessment

Reynell Developmental Language Scales
Chronological Age: 3 years 7 months.
Comprehension: 2 year level.
Expression: 2 years 2 months.

Derbyshire Language Scheme
Chronological Age: 3 years 7 months.
Comprehension: 2 information carrying words.
Chronological Age: 3 years 10 months.
Comprehension: 3 information carrying words.

These scores indicate that Jason's language development, encompassing both comprehension and expression, are delayed. His speech is generally easy to understand.

There is evidence of echolalia and the higher Reynell score for expression reflects the learnt language and situation speech which is typical of Jason's output. However, more importantly, Jason's communication skills are limited and he does not seem able to initiate social communication or devise other means of communication to compensate for deficiencies in his spoken language, i.e. gesture or mime, etc.

Verbal concepts when taught tend to be context bound and Jason's ability to generalise is restricted. He appears to have difficulty extracting implications from situations unless they are of a concrete nature or familiar to him. Jason is reported to be good at doing jigsaws. In school, he can sound words out and match them to objects. He can name colours successfully and is capable of 1:1 correspondence (beginning to understand the nature of number). Nevertheless, in tasks involving classification skills, i.e. sorting, he requires 'cueing in', to enable him to understand the essence of the task.

Progress

Jason has made progress with his listening skills. His comprehension of language has improved, as well as his ability and willingness to communicate. Progress has also been made with verbal concepts. Two months ago Jason was completely unable to draw and held his pen with an immature grasp which is now less in evidence. He responded to verbal directions, i.e. 'Draw a head', 'Where do the eyes go?', etc. and, having 'learnt' to draw a man, persisted in a very stereotyped way and refused to try and draw anything else. After a fortnight's holiday, he had forgotten much of the routine and the man he now persistently draws is minus many of the attributes which he had presumably previously memorised.

Conclusions

It is apparent that Jason's difficulties do not relate simply to delayed language development, but are of a more complex nature relating to social development. These difficulties encompass relationship, communication and understanding and imagination. This suggests a very mild form of autism.

Update

Jason continued to make good progress. His entry into mainstream school was deferred for a few months, during which time he received speech and language therapy. It was apparent that his cognitive development was satisfactory and it was for this reason that the school was not advised of the precise nature of his difficulties. It was felt that a diagnostic label would in no way ease Jason's path, since there was a very good chance that he would succeed in mainstream education without any special provision. Jason settled into his primary school quite happily. He has made good academic progress and has become particularly skilled at reading, though it is evident that he does not understand when the meaning is embedded or implied. However, his social difficulties are of some concern to the school. It is evident that he does not always understand what is expected of him, and in the playground he is usually on the periphery of games and activities and is 'used' by older children as a patient/baby, etc. When the others lose interest, he is unable to initiate a new activity for himself, but is prepared to join in rough and tumble games.

It is hoped that Jason will continue in mainstream education. His intellectual capabilities enable him to learn at least some of the subtle rules of social functioning, though life may not always be very easy for him.

Sean: now aged 4 years 2 months

This report was written when Sean was 2 years 2 months.

Referral and background information

Sean is Jason's younger brother. He was referred for speech and language therapy by his mother when he was under 2 years, as language was not developing. Ironically he had been seen well before his second birthday, during the time that Jason was receiving speech and language therapy. With hindsight, it was unfortunate that more attention was not focused on Sean's early development in the light of what later became so apparent. What can be recalled is the fact that Sean appeared to be very robust compared with his brother. When given free rein, Sean crawled and later walked off in a seemingly purposeful manner, but did not in fact engage in any meaningful activity. He appeared unconcerned about leaving his mother and showed no interactive communication.

At 1 year 10 months, autistic features were observed by the speech and language therapist who carried out a developmental assessment. It was evident that Sean was delayed in all areas and particularly in relation to communication.

Early developmental history

It was reported that the pregnancy and birth were normal and that there were no feeding difficulties. Developmental milestones appear to have been within normal limits. There were indications that all was not well, in that Sean attended more to lights and things that glittered, rather than to people. Sean does not alert to speech, even to his name being called, but a hearing loss has been excluded.

Appearance and behaviour

Superficially, Sean presents as a normal child. However, closer observation reveals not only general immaturity but aspects of deviant development. His looking behaviour is fleeting and eye contact occurs only if his interest is engaged. When left to his own devices, Sean wanders about aimlessly, often holding a car in his hand. He has an interest in cars and will run them up and down and spin the wheels. Hand flapping is in evidence and there is a lack of body language. He often uses peripheral vision, eyeing mainly lights; rapid head shaking, combined with an oblique upward gaze, has also been observed and he appears to be doing this for reasons of self-stimulation rather than negative expression. Unless controlled, Sean will run off, showing no awareness; he does not appear to mind being left and will go to strangers. Generally his behaviour could be described as passive and much of the activity he engages in is purposeless and repetitive, e.g. opening and closing doors. He very much enjoys physical movement, such as swings and slides, as well as general rough and tumble play. He will, however, sit down and watch children's programmes on television.

Sociability

Sean makes his needs known by pulling at an adult. According to his mother he likes being with other children but has very little social understanding indeed. He will seek out physical contact and enjoys being cuddled. His mother remarked, 'He is in his own little world'.

General management and problems

Little progress has been made with toilet training. Sean sleeps very well and has recently started to feed himself. He does not present any management problems and his mother describes him as 'very good'. However, his failure to advance and show motivation causes parental concern and his mother observed that considerable input is required to get any response from him.

Attention control

This is generally fleeting and highly distractable. He shows rigid attention when playing with cars which, as already mentioned, are of considerable interest to him.

Assessment of sensory function

Visual

It was not possible to persuade Sean to co-operate in assessment. He will, however, place one beaker on top of another when his mother facilitates the activity.

Auditory

Sean enjoys toys which play tunes, despite the fact that he does not alert to the human voice.

Proximal senses

Sean still mouths objects.

Communication

Eye contact often occurs but it is fleeting – he will look at an adult for a response if he is disobeying. Generally Sean will not attend to the speech of others, unless the context is clear and of interest to him. On the expressive side, Sean will shake his head for refusal. There is some intonated babble, but generally he is fairly silent, though he has at times echoed single words.

Conclusions

The pattern of development described in this report indicates not only developmental delay but suggests in addition an autistic impairment.

Update

Since this report was written, Sean made slow but steady progress, although he became less easy to manage. He developed food fads and temper tantrums. He was subsequently referred to a consultant paediatrician who could find no evidence of neurological signs nor any syndrome, although it was not possible to carry out any metabolic investigations.

At the age of 3 years 8 months he entered an autistic unit attached to a school for children with severe learning difficulties, where he continues to make progress. A recent developmental assessment has indicated that his self-care skills are within normal limits. Locomotor, manipulative and visual skills are still somewhat delayed. Social development and communication skills remain severely impaired. On assessment, Sean functions at approximately a two and a half year level, but an increase in his use of learnt phrases enables him to function more successfully in everyday situations than formal assessment results suggest. Sean no longer presents in the same robust way and is now a somewhat oddly proportioned little boy.

Freddie: now aged 4 years 6 months

Referral

Freddie was referred to a clinical psychologist by his nursery, with the agreement of his parents, when his behaviour, which was aggressive and destructive, did not show any improvement. He was subsequently referred to an autistic unit for initial assessment. This report was written when Freddie was 4 years 3 months.

Background information

Both parents are high school teachers and Freddie has an older brother in mainstream education who is reported to have had some early difficulties in relation to social development. No details are available. At the age of 2 years 6 months Freddie began attending a nursery. After a few months it was apparent that he would not settle and he was difficult to contain. A place was found for him at another nursery, where the staff have had some experience of children with special needs. The nursery is able to contain him, albeit on Freddie's own terms, so that other children are not too disturbed by his behaviour.

Developmental history

The pregnancy was normal and, despite some distress during labour, Freddie's early months were uneventful and no developmental abnormalities were observed. Apart from the fact that Freddie walked at 10 months, neither parent was able to recall any details of his early development and had particular difficulty with questions relating to his early sociability. He was, however, described as a good baby. At the age of 2 years, however, Freddie became very active indeed. He would run around in circles and was destructive and aggressive. The range and scope of this behaviour extended sufficiently to make family life very difficult. However, Freddie's parents attributed all the mayhem to the notion that it was normal for a boy, and the behaviour was seen in terms of being naughty and seeking attention.

General observations

Freddie's appearance is normal and attractive. He has a somewhat intense gaze, as though he is trying to ascertain the effects of his behaviour. He is able to use language to communicate his needs and interests, but it is not possible to engage him in interactive conversation.

When observed in the nursery, he moved about the room being a tractor, and making engine noises; this activity was sustained for much of the morning. Freddie appeared uninterested in other children and made no attempt to join in their activities. Indeed, his disregard was so great that he was seen to walk over their legs and feet as he wandered about muttering to himself. He did not engage in any purposeful activity and attempts to persuade him to join a group were met with an aggressive outburst, which resulted in him lying on the floor and pulling a picture off the wall and tearing it up. When approached during this activity, Freddie's response was 'Are you going to start the engine?'. At home, however, Freddie occupies himself mainly out of sight but he will play, albeit in a limited way, with such things as a road lay-out.

Assessment

On the second occasion that Freddie was seen, he co-operated very well in the activities that were presented. He was able to match shapes and do simple jigsaws, but used only trial and error tactics. He sniffed many of the pieces before using them. Although Freddie could match colours using like objects, he had difficulty when the objects were different – likewise with shape. He could match objects to pictures, but not pictures to objects, despite a demonstration. A later attempt to continue the assessment resulted in a demonstration of wild behaviour, when Freddie pinched the clinician, pulled hair, tore up papers, threw objects out of the window and even bit her.

Discussion

Freddie's range of developmental problems suggest that autism is a relevant context in which to consider his management and educational needs. It is not helpful to regard his behaviour as simply naughty and attention seeking. This diverts attention from his underlying difficulties, and disregards the many indications that the problems are more wide-ranging and complex.

Although Freddie shows some social awareness, he does not show social understanding and appears uninterested and unconcerned about the needs of others, unless they coincide with his own. His interests are circumscribed and he does not show appropriate imagination and creativity. It is felt that he is not well managed at home, but it would be simplistic to attribute such serious behavioural problems to bad management alone.

Update

The very experienced clinical psychologist involved with this little boy considered that a diagnosis of deviant autism would account for his problems and extreme behaviour. These certainly encompass the essential areas of Lorna Wing's triad. Yet the parents were angry and outraged at the diagnosis and refused to accept her views. Although they do now acknowledge that Freddie has special needs, a suitable educational placement is likely to be hard to find because of the severity of his behaviour difficulties. The situation remains unresolved.

Fiona: now aged 8 years

Referral

Fiona was referred to a specialist speech and language therapist from the community as a deviant pattern of language delay was recognised. This report was written when Fiona was 6 years of age, a year after the initial referral.

Backgound information

Fiona is the younger of two children. Her sister is normal and attends a mainstream school.

Developmental history

Fiona was a full-term baby and was born after a long labour. From birth she screamed a great deal, slept very little and was not a good feeder. Weight gain was slow and she had constant diarrhoea. Both parents felt that something was wrong, especially as it was almost impossible to comfort her. Numerous medical consultations proved ineffective in providing any relief until her mother, through a support group for parents of hyperactive children, was put in touch with a practitioner with an interest in dietary/metabolic causes of behavioural difficulties. His investigations revealed that Fiona was severely deficient in zinc.

At about the same time, it was observed that Fiona was suffering from spasmodic episodes, mainly at night, when her body was seen to shake and her eyes deviate. Epilin was prescribed for what was considered to be an epileptic condition. The parents were reluctant to give Fiona this drug as she was about to commence treatment with zinc. Following the administration of zinc, there was an immediate and dramatic change in Fiona's sleeping pattern and a subsequent improvement in her behaviour. As well as the zinc treatment, dairy products and artificial additives were excluded from her diet; she was also given vitamin supplements. No further episodes were reported and, according to her mother, recent neurological examination has not revealed any abnormalities (see *Update*).

Recently, however, Fiona's behaviour at home has reverted. She sleeps very litle at night and this appears not to have any deleterious effect on her energy output during the day. She is a very difficult child to manage at home and causes considerable disruption to other members of the family.

General observations

Fiona is small for her age. She has good eye contact and an alert, enquiring facial expression which, together with a remarkable lexicon of social chat, gives an impression of greater ability than is subsequently revealed by close examination. Fiona's present appearance and happy demeanour do not compare with the way she presented less than a year ago, when her waif-like figure and anxious facial expression were not enhanced by a 'tonsure' on the crown of her head where she had pulled out her hair. Apart from a tendency to lick her chin excessively, causing almost constant soreness, her appearance is essentially normal.

In school, Fiona is easy to manage, which is in contrast to the management problems she presents at home. Her repertoire of behavioural characteristics are, at the present time, perseverative, rather than bizarre. However, it is worth mentioning that the range of abnormalities was greater when Fiona was younger, which is of diagnostic significance. These included body spinning, hair pulling, resistance to change, unreasonable fears, distress caused by certain sounds, temper tantrums and an insistence on undressing herself, a skill which she was able to execute with remarkable speed. Most of these behaviours have disappeared or diminished considerably.

When left to her own devices, Fiona's general activity could be described as aimless. She has a particular interest in clothes and shoes and shows a remarkable ability to remember the appearance of cars belonging to people known to her.

Within the context of her difficulties, Fiona gets pleasure from being with people. She is very adept at knowing how to annoy others and uses this ability with considerable effect at home.

Within the classroom group, she will join in with the games of other, socially normal children, but is unable to initiate meaningful play herself. Her own play is symbolic, but she cannot develop her play imaginatively and creatively.

Although Fiona's self-care skills are age appropriate, she still wets at night and has to wear a nappy.

Attention control

This is at a single channel level, which indicates that Fiona can attend to an adult's choice of activity but her attention is difficult to control.

Sensory function

Visual perception

This is not an area of relative ability and her skills are not age appropriate.

Auditory perception

This area of functioning is undoubtedly an 'islet of ability'. In all aspects of auditory skills, Fiona exhibits a level of capability in excess of her general level of development.

Body awareness

Fiona functions well in this sphere and shows good co-ordination.

Proximal senses

Fiona likes to smell people and food; she shows a normal awareness of heat, cold, pain, etc.

Non-verbal symbolic function

As mentioned earlier, Fiona plays symbolically and can be drawn into the games of other children. She is also able to role play in a limited imitative way, according to her mother who has described Fiona's actions with a toy microphone.

In all her play activities, however, Fiona is unable to develop beyond a certain level.

Concept formation

Although Fiona can match objects according to different criteria, her classification skills are limited to colour. Her verbal concepts are limited and are not age appropriate.

Sequencing and rhythmic abilities

Visual

This is not an area of special competence.

Auditory

Fiona is good at dancing, which is an activity she enjoys. She is able to extricate complex rhythm sequences in music and clap them with accuracy.

Speech and Language

Comprehension

In this area Fiona has considerable difficulty, which becomes very apparent on assessment.

In day-to-day situations, provided that the language and context which act as a 'trigger' are familiar, Fiona is able to respond deceptively well. However, when the wrong triggers are provided, comprehension breaks down and it is not possible to pursue a conversation with her; she is unable to utilise semantic information. In a limited way, Fiona demonstrates a sense of humour.

Expression

Fiona has a remarkable ability to recall and imitate the speech of others. She constantly talks and mutters to herself and it is possible to pick out the 'ownership' of her utterances. Provided the appropriate triggers are delivered by the listener, Fiona is able to use her echolalia to communicate, and this ability elevates her social functioning considerably, giving, as mentioned earlier, a false impression of her capabilities. When conversation is attempted beyond the confines of her interests or immediate experience, she will quickly resort to stereotyped repetitions and it becomes obvious that she is unable to communicate normally. Generally, Fiona will readily respond verbally but the content of her utterances, though linguistically intact, is more often than not irrelevant to the situation. Remarkably, Fiona can manipulate language grammatically, whether or not meaning is attached to what she is saying. Fiona's articulation and vocal delivery sound very mature; this also enhances expectations of her abilities and provides a very misleading impression.

Educational Attainments

Although Fiona attempts to 'write', there is little progress in the acquisition of literacy and numeracy skills.

Results of Assessments

Reynell Developmental Language Scales – 26.11.87
Chronological age: 5 years 6 months.
Comprehension: 2 years 9 months.
Expression: 2 years 7/8 months.

Derbyshire Language Scheme – 24.9.87
Chronological age: 5 years 4 months.
Comprehension: 2/3 information carrying words.

Schedule of Handicaps Behaviour and Skills (Wing MRC) – July 1987
Chronological age: 5 years 2 months.
A developmental profile shows clearly that Fiona's level of functioning in areas other than self-care and gross motor skills are well below her chronological age.

Sheridan – November 1987
Chronological age: 5 years 6 months.
Posture and large movements: 4 years 6 months.
Fine motor: 3 years.
Hearing and speech: 2 years 9 months.
Social behaviour and play: 2 years 9 months.

Overall, Fiona presents as a 2 years 6 months/3 year old, apart from gross motor.

Diagnosis

The spectrum of behavioural and learning difficulties which Fiona presents indicates that autism is an appropriate context in which to consider them – indeed the conflicting pattern of her developmental profile and history is very common in autistic children. Although by no means a classic 'Kanner Type', Fiona's autistic features, together with possible metabolic factors, demonstrate a familiar pattern within the autistic continuum. It is worth noting that Fiona's initial dramatic response to the administration of zinc, mirrors similar dramatic improvements in other children treated with a range of drugs, including fenfluramine, vitamin B6, as well as mega-vitamin therapy.

Over the years, Fiona's parents have seen a number of doctors in a quest for an answer, if not a cure, for Fiona's difficulties. This has not happened and, most surprisingly, when a diagnosis of autism was made by Dr X in 1986, the parents were not told. Ultimately it was the school which informed the parents that Fiona's difficulties were of an autistic nature and the autistic continuum was discussed.

Although the parents were most upset and at the time confused by the diagnosis, believing that Fiona simply had a language disorder, they have since become reconciled and have a better understanding of the implications of Fiona's deficits and difficulties.

Update

Since this report was written, Fiona's behaviour has had its ups and downs, and she has continued to be a difficult child to manage at home. However, overall there has been steady improvement. Shortly after the report was written, when Fiona was over 6 years of age, a paediatric department of another teaching hospital finally discovered a genetic condition which is frequently linked to autism as well as mental handicap. This was present from birth, but went unrecognised. Because of the presence of a known condition, the effectiveness or otherwise of the zinc supplements cannot be evaluated.

Fiona's physical condition improved dramatically once a sensible eating programme had been introduced at school. Her appearance changed dramatically. The Dickensian waif was replaced by a robust child, who could best be described by the epithet 'bright eyed and bushy tailed'. One year later, Fiona's comprehension of language had improved more than could be accounted for by maturation. Although on formal assessment her score for expressive language was not much in excess of her level of understanding, the language which she generated herself on topics which interested her was considerably better. Her capability with spoken language is in fact quite remarkable and may be regarded as an islet of ability. However, Fiona's skill in using language for interactive communication, when she has not chosen the topic, remains extremely limited.

Now, at the age of 8 years, Fiona has made satisfactory progress in educational terms, given that she has marked learning difficulties, particularly in areas of development which relate to the acquisition of number concepts. She has been able to make a start in the core areas of the National Curriculum. Fiona's play with other children is participatory and, within the limits of her social skills, gains maximum benefit from contact with other children, although in a wider mainstream setting she is not yet able to cope satisfactorily. Fiona's communication skills are entirely equivocal. On the one hand, she is an excellent communicator, her body language is normal and she gets great pleasure and enjoyment from group language sessions – both from listening and communicating herself. Yet her ability to use language creatively remains limited. She has a good vocabulary and it is certainly true that at times she can say absolutely the right thing, often with appropriate humour. However, her underlying difficulties emerge, despite her lively personality, her zest and interest in the world about her.

It is apparent from these observations that Fiona's autism has receded, which is not to say that her difficulties are over, but it does indicate how well autistic children can progress and what enjoyment and pleasure they can provide.

A MOTHER'S STORY

This poignant account written by the mother of a young autistic child vividly describes her experiences as she struggled to find out what was the matter, and how to help her son. Although we have minimally edited the narrative, changed names and disguised locations, the text is essentially as it was written. We are grateful to this parent for allowing us to present her story.

'You have asked for a profile to the best of my knowledge on Scott's five years which he will be on 10th April 1990. I will do this profile with all honesty and to the nearest and most accurate as I can. I will start from 0–6 months, then 6–12 months and 12–24 months etc.

'Starting with 0–6 months. Scott was born on 10th April 1985. From the time I was expecting to when he was born I felt really well and his birth was normal, drug-free except for gas and air. When he was born, he was 7lbs 6ozs and healthy. I was also fine. He was a really good baby. You would call him an angel because he was such a quiet baby. He would sleep, feed, then sleep and feed. This went on until he was 6 months, when he did not need so much sleep. Around 6–7 months, he would just sit in his baby bouncer for hours, not really looking at anything or taking much interest in anyone. When Scott got to about 11–12 months, all he used to do was cry a lot. He still did not take much notice of anything and as a mother I really thought he did not like me much. He was very spiteful and distant, and what I noticed the most at this time was an incredible anxiety with his personality. It was terrible. He showed this with anybody and everything, especially with me, maybe because I was with him all day and I was his lifeline. If he got frustrated, he would take it out on me.

'Around 12–24 months. He started walking at 17 months, but did not venture much as another baby would when starting to walk. Scott would walk around in a kind of routine. What I mean is, he would walk from the front room into one bedroom, out again to the other bedroom, then into the bathroom, then the toilet and then the kitchen. He would do this for hours, just walking in and out of the rooms. His behaviour if you tried to distract him would be crazy. He would scream and cry so bad it was like you were trying to kill him. I would try and play with him with toys, books, etc. but he would not do anything with me. He would throw cars, toys, bottles. Anything he could get his hands on would be aimed at me. He would not look at me or anyone else. He would not make any eye contact.

'Age 24 months–3 years. Scott was I would say at his worst. I could not take him out anywhere. I became like a prisoner in my own home. It was at this stage, when he was so bad, I must admit I thought he was a little crazy and I knew he was not getting any better, and he didn't have any speech. A lot of outsiders were more worried about his speech and thought, if his speech was better, so would his behaviour be better. But I knew as a mother and living with Scott twenty-four hours a day, that there was more to it than speech and behaviour problems.

'So I heard about autism. I read a lot of books and had seen a few programmes on telly but what I had read and seen, and the people I had seen and read about were so severe, I thought Scott can't be autistic because he was not as bad as that. But always in my heart, I still thought well maybe just slightly autistic. Anyway, people said, "No way". So I pushed it to the back of my mind and coped to the best I could. Scott at this stage, just destroyed everything he got his hands on. He would not listen to anything or anyone. He could also sit for hours, looking at the carpet, but was not looking at it. He seemed to go into a trance, and if you would try and distract him from his trance, he would hit, bite, scream, throw objects, go crazy. You would really have to let Scott have his own way and let him do his own thing to a certain extent. This way, I could get more peace, to go on with life. He was just like a loner, in his own world, and who didn't want to be distracted.

'At 3 years 6 months, when he started nursery it was terrible. The teachers had a terrible time. They did not know where to begin. He would not do anything he was told. They asked on a few occasions about did he hear properly. He would not mix with his peers, or could not! Nobody could understand what he was saying, because he sounded dumb and could not speak anyway. I could understand Scott more, because I was with him all day and got to know his language. I could also feel his emotions – sounds crazy, but I could feel his needs mentally and understand to a great length what he wanted or did not. At nursery, his behaviour remained the same, destructive, throwing tantrums, screaming, crying. He would not listen to any story. He would do what he wanted to do and at any time he wanted to do it. The teachers did their best, but were also tried and tested with Scott and were at a loss because they did not know how to treat him. So they did their best to stop him harming himself and others, and trying their best to get him to join in. They have been brilliant and done very well with him.

'Three to 4 years 6 months. Scott was still bad at 3 years 6 months, but was now able to sit and do more. For instance, he would watch videos for about two hours, but you were not allowed to sit with him, touch him, kiss or cuddle him. He hated any physical emotion. But towards being 4 years 6 months, he was improving greatly. I would make him sit, kiss, love, touch, cry, smell, and feel, until he would respond. This was a great help, but at first he was so bad, he would go crazy, really, really bad. It hurt me to see Scott suffering, but I had no choice. What else could I do? I had a son who needed help and I was the only one who would or could help him.

'Also at home, he would only need about 6 hours sleep. He always went to bed at 8 o'clock in the evening, then awake around 2–3 o'clock in the morning and just destroy everything. He would rip wallpaper, pull everything out of kitchen cupboards, pour milk all over the floor, flood the bathroom. One day he found paint, poured it all over the hall carpet, and all over the walls in the bathroom. My opinion was, still autistic and also speech frustrations very bad, and anxiety as well.

'I hope by now you have got a general picture of Scott's behaviour and speech. So I will continue with my worry about education. I am really worried about Scott's understanding. He cannot understand anything he has not already learned. For example, if you say to Scott, "How old are you? Where do you live?", he cannot answer, because he does not understand. He has no concept of numbers. Well, he has no concept of anything really. I have drummed into Scott everything I can and his improvement in the last eight months is remarkable. Eight months ago he could do nothing. He could not speak. He had totally no understanding at all. So I thought to myself, well, if I don't help, nobody will. So I bought books, and toys, and sat down with Scott and worked very hard to make him listen, play and read to him, talk with him. What I did, was not to give in to him any more. I gave nothing to Scott's demands. I let him scream, cry, throw tantrums, hit out at me. It took months before any progress was seen. But Scott saw that I was not going to give in, so after having a very hard battle of wills, I was finally winning, and Scott finally started to stop crying and screaming, and slowly listened to me. And then, because he was so behind, it also took a lot of patience to teach Scott.

'I started with words like cat, dog, etc. and a b c d e, etc. And then talked to him, like saying, "Look at the water coming out of the tap", and then saying, "The reason why we wash is to get clean, because dirty looks silly." I tried to explain reasons why about everything, so he started to get more involved. For instance, if a cat was meowing, I would say to Scott without him even being interested, "Scott, listen to that cat, he is crying because he wants some dinner." I would say this about twelve times, before he could take it in, or even be interested. I would never ever stop talking or singing and acting as he would like me to. I was always trying to be funny, and he would love me being funny. If he showed interest in anything, I would always let him look, listen and join in, with him acting as he would.

'By now, Scott became very close to me. A miracle was, he showed me love, kissed and always cuddled me. I was so happy. He also now wanted to kiss everybody and has a great love for other children. His teachers at school, who he has now known for nearly two years, he loves, and his brothers. He has two brothers. Steve, he loves very much. Steve is 11 in September, and has always treated Scott normally and protected him. But Steve gets very frustrated at times with Scott, because how do you explain to an 11-year-old, about Scott's mentality? He sees Scott as normal, which is good. Scott also has a baby brother called Paul, who he adores, but does not like the baby to touch him, and kiss and cuddle him.

'Scott has a cousin called Marie. He hated her at first until he reached about 3 years old. Now he will play with Marie more than his brothers or children at school. He will share most things with her, but there are times when he still won't talk or play or kiss with anyone. Unless Scott wants to, the only one he will love and protect at all times is myself, his mother.

'Scott, as he is today. Scott is so different these days you would think he was a new boy from a year ago. He can now talk in little sentences to me. He can make eye contact. He can show anger, fear, love, kindness as well. He can show almost every emotion as a normal child. But my biggest worry is his understanding. He can only understand what I have taught him. His mind is just like a video recorder, only remembering the input which he has learned, and beyond this, he does not know or understand. He does not know why we eat, drink, laugh, and sleep. He has no concept for money. He does not know why we have to pay for everything in shops, why his brothers have different ages, or why his baby brother cannot speak yet and why his baby brother does not understand him when Scott talks to him or wants him to do something. Scott still gets very aggressive and has tantrums still. He will not listen or try to learn songs and stories, unless it's what he wants, and then it all depends on what mood he is in.

'Scott is now very loving, but I have noticed over the last couple of weeks, Scott is only very loving and kind to the people who spoil or give in to him. I find this quite upsetting, because people who don't let him have his way, he will say to me, or the person concerned, "Scott is not your friend." He is quite aggressive towards them. I am the only person who is very strict and firm with Scott and he still loves me very much, although he gets very hurt, and sometimes if I have been very firm, this shatters Scott's emotions so much he gets very depressed. Scott's personality is so very hard to cope with. He wants attention from me all the time, and always has got to be the centre of everything. At the moment he is more demanding which may be because my baby son Paul is taking up a lot of my time now he is getting older. It is hard to judge.

'Since I started writing this, Scott's speech and understanding has greatly improved and I am quite surprised.

'The main worry is I do not think he is ready for mainstream school. He cannot understand well enough to go to mainstream, or speak well enough. He cannot dress himself well enough. He cannot feed himself (or maybe he is just lazy!). I feed him at home, because he will not eat unless I feed him, and then it's a battle, because Scott has a terrible appetite. He hardly eats anything. He cannot or won't wash himself. I still wash him. I mainly do everything for Scott, so I am worried about when he goes to school. He will not be able to sit in a classroom full of children, because he will not understand hardly anything which is being said. He understands a lot better, but with great difficulty. For instance, when I am washing him in the morning, and I pull the plug out, he will say, "Mum, where is the water going?" I say, "Down the pipes, because it's dirty water". He will say, "Why is it dirty?" I will say, "Because your hands and face were dirty, we wash them with the water, so now it's dirty water". "Why is it dirty water?" etc. etc. This can go on and on for about ten to fifteen minutes, until he gets fed up. But he still doesn't really understand why. He just gets fed up and goes off.

'But to finish off, Scott is very clever and even crafty, and knows a lot more than he lets on. I do not know why this is so, maybe it's his personality. He pretends or hides his true ability to a certain extent, but my last word is, he is not clever enough for mainstream schooling. All I know is, there is something wrong in most areas which needs special attention.'

Scott's mother unfortunately received shamefully little help and support during his pre-school years. It was not until Scott was over 5 years of age that he was correctly diagnosed, and appropriate educational placement offered.

Scott now attends a special unit for children with autistic features. He is very happy and is making good progress.

Appendix 2

USEFUL CONTACTS AND ADDRESSES

This appendix is addressed to parents of young children who are beginning to think that their child is not developing normally, and have an inkling that he or she could be autistic. Perhaps they have already consulted their family doctor and been encouraged to stop worrying, and yet doubts remain. They feel embarrassed about making a return visit with their healthy and attractive child, and hate the idea of being labelled as a fussy parent. What, in these circumstances, is the best thing to do? We would suggest that first of all they contact their Health Visitor. It is apparent that many families lose touch with their Health Visitor after their child's very early infancy, especially when all seems satisfactory and the mother is coping well. When the autistic features emerge, often as late as the child's third year, there is no immediate professional to turn to and it is difficult for parents to know what to do, let alone how to evaluate their child's difficulties.

Another course of action is to make direct contact with the local Community Speech and Language Therapy Service. It is not necessary to have a doctor's referral, simply contact the District Speech and Language Therapist asking for a consultation. Although there is a national shortage of speech and language therapists, sooner or later an appointment will be made available. Speech and Language Therapists, even if they have little, if any, experience of the condition of autism, are trained to assess a child's overall communication skills in relation to development. As a professional group, they are the most likely to offer support. In recent years they have started to play an increasingly important role in the recognition and assessment of autism in young children.

Although the speech and language therapist may be the most useful professional contact for parents in this situation, they should not necessarily assume that a course of treatment will be offered. What is most likely is that their child will be assessed, possibly over a number of weeks. It will be this assessment which will hopefully enable parents to begin to understand their puzzling child and additionally provide indicators for future management and appropriate onward referral.

Advisory Centre for
Education
18 Victoria Park Square
London E2 9PB
Tel: 081–980 4596

The Association of Head
Teachers of Autistic Children
and Adults
1 Aston Road
London W5 2RL
Tel: 081–998 2700

Autism Research Review
International
Institute for Child Behavior
Research
Director: Bernard Rimland
4182 Adams Avenue
San Diego, California 92116
USA

Autism Research Unit
School of Pharmaceutical
and Chemical Sciences
Faculty of Science
Sunderland Polytechnic
Sunderland SR2 7EE
Tel: 091–510 8922
Fax: 091–515 2557 (marked:
Autism Research Unit)

Contact-a-Family
16 Strutton Ground
London SW1 2HP
Tel: 071–222 2695
Information available about
their availability nationwide

The Handicapped
Adventure Playground
Association (HAPA)
Fulham Palace
Bishops Avenue
London SW6 6EA
Tel: 071–736 4443
Facilities in Inner and
Greater London, but
Information Officer will
provide information about
associated schemes in other
areas

Mencap
Mencap National Centre
123 Golden Lane
London EC1
Tel: 071–253 9433

National Association for
Remedial Education (NARE)
Central Office
2 Lichfield Road
Stafford ST17 4JX
Publications available,
including *Word Play*
(Wolfendale and Bryans
1986)

The National Autistic Society
276 Willesden Lane
London NW2 5RB
Tel: 081–451 1114

The National Portage
Association
Secretary: Mollie White
4 Clifton Road
Winchester
Hants
Tel: 0962–60148

References and further reading

Aarons, M. and Gittens, T. (1987) *Is This Autism?*, Windsor: NFER-Nelson.

Aarons, M. and Gittens, T. (1990) 'What is the True Essence of Autism?', *Speech Therapy in Practice*, 5.8.

Aarons, M. and Gittens, T. (1991) 'Higashi or Home?', *Therapy Weekly*, 17.31.

Association of Head Teachers of Autistic Children and Adults (1985), *The Special Curricular Needs of Autistic Children*, London: Association of Head Teachers of Autistic Children and Adults.

Association of Head Teachers of Autistic Children and Adults (1990) *The Special Curricular Needs of Autistic Children: Learning and Thinking Skills*, London: Association of Head Teachers of Autistic Children and Adults.

Baron-Cohen, S. (1988) 'Social and Pragmatic Deficits in Autism: Cognitive or Affective?', *Journal of Autism and Developmental Disorders*, 18.3.

Bishop, D. (1983) *Test For Reception of Grammar (TROG)*, Manchester: Department of Psychology, University of Manchester.

Bishop, D. (1989) 'Autism, Asperger's Syndrome and Semantic-pragmatic Disorder: Where are the Boundaries?', *British Journal of Disorders of Communication*, 24.2.

Carr, J. (1980) *Helping Your Handicapped Child: A Penguin Handbook*, Harmondsworth: Penguin.

Christie, P. (1987) 'Holding Therapy', *Communication*, 21.3.

Christie, P., Newson, E., Newson, J. and Prevezer, W. (in press) 'An Interactive Approach to Language and Communication for Non-speaking Children: Practical Guidelines from a Developmental Standpoint', *Handbook of Child and Adolescent Therapy in Britain*, Milton Keynes: Open University Press.

Cooper, J., Moodley, M. and Reynell, J. (1978) *Helping Language Development*, London: Edward Arnold.

Dewart H. and Summers, S. (1988) *The Pragmatics Profile of Early Communication Skills*, Windsor: NFER-Nelson.

Elgar, S. (1985) 'Sex Education and Sexual Awareness Building for Autistic Children and Youth: Some Viewpoints and Considerations', *Journal of Autism and Developmental Disorders*, 15. 2.

Ellis, K. (ed.) (1990) *Autism, Professional Perspectives and Practice*, London: Chapman & Hall in association with the National Autistic Society.

Frith, U. (1989) *Autism: Explaining the Enigma*, Oxford: Blackwell.

Frith, U. (ed.)(1991) *Autism and Asperger Syndrome*, Cambridge: Cambridge University Press.

Gilby, K., Jones, G. and Newson, E. (1988) 'Autistic Children in Ordinary Mainstream Schools', Summary Report DHSS/DES Research Project, Child Development Research Unit, University of Nottingham.

Gillberg, C. (1990) 'Autistic and Pervasive Developmental Disorders', *Journal of Child Psychology and Psychiatry*, 31. 1.

Gillberg, C., Ehlers, S., Schaumann, H., Jakobsson, G., Dahlgren, S.O., Lindblom, R., Bågenholm, A., Tjuus, T. and Blidner, E. (1990) 'Autism Under Age 3 Years: A Clinical Study of 28 Cases Referred for Autistic Symptoms in Infancy', *Journal of Child Psychology and Psychiatry*, 31.6.

Grandin, T. and Scariano, M. (1986) *Emergence Labelled Autistic*, Tunbridge Wells: D. J. Costello (Publishers) Ltd.

Howlin, P. (1987) 'Commissioned Review – Autism', Newsletter, Association of Child Psychology and Psychiatry, 9.4.

Howlin, P. (1989) 'Living with Impairment: The Effects on Children of having an Autistic Sibling', *Child: Care, Health and Development*, 14, 395–408.

Kanner, L. (1943) 'Autistic Disturbances of Affective Contact', *Nervous Child*, 2.217.

Knowles, W. and Masidlover, M. (1980) *Derbyshire Language Scheme*, Ripley: Derbyshire County Council Education Psychology Service.

Lowe, M. and Costello, A. J. (1976) *Symbolic Play Test*, Windsor: NFER-Nelson.

Miedzianik, D. (1986) *My Autobiography*, Nottingham: Child Development Research Unit, University of Nottingham.

Morton, J. (1989) 'The Origins of Autism', *New Scientist*, December 1989, also in *Communication*, 24.3, December 1990.

National Autistic Society (1991) *Dictionary of Approaches to Autism: An Annotated List*, London: National Autistic Society.

Newson, E., Dawson, M. and Everard, P. (1984) 'The Natural History of Able Autistic People: Their Management and Functioning in a Social Context', Summary of the Report to the DHSS, Communication, Vol. XVIII, Nos. 1, 2, 3, 4 and Vol. XIX, Nos. 1, 2, London: National Autistic Society.

Renfrew, C. (1989) 'Action Picture Test', IIIrd Edition, and 'The Bus Story', (1990), IIIrd Edition, obtainable from C. Renfrew, North Place, Old Headington, Oxford.

Reynell, J. (1985) *The Reynell Developmental Language Scales*, (Second Revision), Windsor: NFER-Nelson.

Rimland, B. (1988) 'Physical Exercise and Autism', *Autism Research Review*, 2.4.

Roberts, J. (1989) 'Echolalia and Comprehension in Autistic Children', *Journal of Autism and Developmental Disorders*, 19.2.

Rutter, M. (1984) 'The Language Development of the Young Autistic Child', in *Autism, its Nature, Implications and Consequences*, London: National Autistic Society.

Rutter, M. (1985) 'The Treatment of Autistic Children', *Journal of Child Psychology and Psychiatry*, 26.2.

Seheult, C. (1990) 'Using Parents as Their Children's Therapists', *Communication*, 24.2.

Selfe, L. (1984) 'Art and Autism', in *Autism, its Nature, Implications and Consequences*, London: National Autistic Society.

Shea, V. and Mesibov, G. (1985) 'The Relationship of Learning Disabilities and Higher-Level Autism', *Journal of Autism and Developmental Disorders*, 15.4.

Tantam, D. (1988) *A Mind of One's Own*, London: National Autistic Society.

Taylor, E. and Hemsley, R. (1990) 'Dietary Treatment in Autism and Hyperactivity', *Communication*, 24.2.

Tinbergen N. and Tinbergen, E. (1984) 'Autistic Children: New Hope for a Cure', London: George Allen & Unwin.

Treffert, D. (1989) *Extraordinary People*, London: Bantam Press, reprinted in paperback in 1990.

Upton, G. (1990) 'The Education Reform Act and Special Educational Needs', Newsletter: Association for Child Psychology and Psychiatry, Vol.12, No.5.

Wiltshire, S. (1989) *Cities*, London: Dent.

Wing, L. (1981) 'Asperger's Syndrome: A Clinical Account', *Journal of Psychological Medicine* 11, 115–129.

Wing, L. (ed.) (1988a) *Aspects of Autism: Biological Research*, London: Gaskell/National Autistic Society.

Wing, L. (1988b) 'The Continuum of Autistic Characteristics', in Schopler, E. and Mesibov, G. (eds) *Diagnosis and Assessment in Autism*, New York: Plenum.

Wing, L. and Gould, J. (1976) 'Systematic Recording of Behaviours and Skills of Retarded and Psychotic Children', *Journal of Autism and Developmental Disorders*, 8.1.

Wing, L. and Gould, J. (1979) 'Severe Impairments of Social Interaction and Associated Abnormalities in Children: Epidemiology and Classification', *Journal of Autism and Developmental Disorders*, 9.1.

Wolfendale, S. and Bryans, T. (1986) *Word Play*, Stafford: NARE Publications.

Wolff, S. *et al.* (1988) 'Personality Characteristics of Parents of Autistic Children: A Controlled Study', *Journal of Psychology and Psychiatry*, 29.2.

Index